The SACRED CENTER

The SACRED CENTER

THE ANCIENT ART OF LOCATING SANCTUARIES

John Michell

Inner Traditions
Rochester, Vermont

Inner Traditions
One Park Street
Rochester, Vermont 05767
www.InnerTraditions.com

Originally published in the United Kingdom in 1994 by Thames and Hudson
Ltd. under the title *At the Centre of the World: Polar Symbolism Discovered in
Celtic, Norse and Other Ritualized Landscapes*

Library of Congress Cataloging-in-Publication Data
Michell, John F.
  [At the center of the world]
  The sacred center : the ancient art of locating sanctuaries / John Michell.
      p. cm.
  Originally published: At the centre of the world : polar symbolism discovered in
Celtic, Norse and other ritualized landscapes. New York : Thames and Hudson,
1994.
  Includes bibliographical references and index.
  ISBN 978-1-59477-284-9
  1. Sacred space. 2. Orientation (Religion) 3. British Isles—Miscellanea. 4.
Faroe Islands—Miscellanea. 5. Mythology, Celtic. 6. Mythology, Norse. I. Title.
  BL980.G7M53 2009
  304.2'3—dc22

                                                                  2008050244

Printed and bound in the United States by Lake Book Manufacturing

10 9 8 7 6 5 4 3 2 1

Text design by Ginny Scott Bowman, layout by Jon Desautels
This book was typeset in Garamond Premier Pro with Schneidler used as display
typeface

To send correspondence to the author of this book, mail a first-class letter to the
author c/o Inner Traditions • Bear & Company, One Park Street, Rochester, VT
05767, and we will forward the communication.

CONTENTS

ACKNOWLEDGMENTS

Curious items of information and hospitality in his travels have been provided by many friends of the author, who thanks them all warmly, with special gratitude to Anabelle Conyngham, Thomas Cowell, Jamie George, the Knight of Glyn, Derham Groves, Desmond and Penny Guinness, Merrily Harpur, Francis Herbert of the Royal Geographical Society, Prudence Jones, Seaver Leslie, Julian and Victoria Lloyd, Glare Lyon, J. E. Neal, Peggy Nugent, Gearoid O'Brien, Keith Payne, Nigel Pennick, Ian Tait of the Lerwick Museum, Bob Trubshaw, and G. V. C. Young.

Thanks above all to Christine Rhone for advice, companionship, and drawing the diagrams.

Acknowledgments are overdue to Thomas Neurath of Thames and Hudson for his encouragement and support of this work and others that led up to it.

I

FINDING THE CENTER

Sitting Around the Fire

If you are calm, clearheaded, and rationally decisive, people say you are well centered or focused. In that saying is our instinctive recognition that everything has its proper center, which is also its essence.

The essence of an individual, one's center and citadel, is the mind. But it is not the ultimate center, and if you think it so, you are properly called self-centered and a solipsist. In that case, life's greater realities pass you by. It is the basic premise of psychology and the only premise that allows the existence of science and the possibility of true knowledge about anything at all—that all minds are of the same stuff and proceed, similarly structured, from the same source. Like every snowflake, which is a unique variation on the same hexagonal theme, every individual mind is a unique reflection of an original, formative pattern. Reflections or copies of anything are naturally less perfect than their prototype, which represents their ideal form. Among the infinite variety of its products, the prototype is the only constant. This corresponds to the relationship between the restless, ever-fluctuating field of human minds and Mind itself.

The idea of a fixed center and a continually moving periphery has many illustrations. It is like a wheel turning on its axle, a rope swung round a vertical pole, a compass making a circle. A grander cosmological image is of a spherical universe, with the spherical Earth at its

1

center, both revolving on the same unmoving pivot, the world-pole.

In all traditional systems of religion, this image has provided the dominant symbol. The doctrine associated with it describes the universe as a divinely born creature, never the same, never at rest, but with a still, unvarying center that, like the core of a magnetic field, governs everything around it.

A natural product of this worldview is a social order that is designed to reflect the order of the universe. It is centered in every sense upon a symbol of the world-pole, which is itself a symbol of eternal law. In imitation of the universal pattern, every unit in society replicates the entire social structure, so an image of the world-pole is found at the center of every community and every household.

In the earliest and perhaps most satisfying form of dwelling, the "primitive hut," the center is located in the middle of the circular room. People sit around the square hearthstone, where the fire warms a round pot suspended on a chain, and smoke ascends through the apex of the conical, thatched roof. Anthropologists say that this practical arrangement is seen in all lands as a cosmological scheme. Within the circumference of the universe, symbolized by the outer wall, the hearthstone is both the body of the earth, with four corners, directions, and yearly seasons, and Hestia, the (h)earth goddess, whose energies are concentrated in the central fire. The cauldron on the fire is also like the earth, a source of comfort and nourishment, and the chain that holds it is the world-pole, the link between heaven and earth and the means of intercourse with gods and spirits. The imagination ascends with the smoke, passes through the hole in the roof, and is free, like the soul of a shaman, to wander where it will. In that situation, sitting with familiar company around a fire on which a pot is simmering, one is likely to feel at ease and well centered.

We still speak of sitting "around" a fire, even though the modern fireplace has been displaced to one side of a rectangular room and we actually sit in front of it. With this new fashion, the old cosmology lost its influence, and it may be that minds became less "centered" thereby. Yet the hearth or fireplace still provided the usual household focus, its ornamented mantle shelf serving as a personal or family altar. Today the flickering television or the electric cooker has become the main focus of many homes.

Thus, the traditional cosmology is no longer represented by its domestic symbols, and a new, secular, restless, uncentered worldview has taken its place.

"Focus," meaning a center that receives and emits rays of light, is the Latin name for the central fireplace. The fire not only warms, but as a symbol, also illuminates the corresponding images of a center to each of our own beings and of a world-center that is divine, eternal, and unchanging.

For calming the mind and restoring it to its natural order, there is no substitute for a centrally placed hearth. There is much comfort in our modern domestic machinery—computers, central heating— but with these accessories we are not exactly focused. We are in fact distracted, torn from the realities of dreams and imaginings centered upon our own hearths and minds, and aimlessly adrift in a sea of alien fantasies.

Modern house builders have given us high levels of convenience and hygiene, while ignoring the psychological necessity of a proper focus; through the absence of a cosmologically significant center, the modern mind has become unbalanced, and we are less able to feel centered.

The Infinity of Centers

At the beginning of his essay "At the Centre of the Earth" in *Architecture, Mysticism and Myth,* W. R. Lethaby wrote, "There would seem to be a delight and mystery inherent to the idea of a boundary or a centre. Children show this by standing in two counties or parishes at the same time, and being much comforted thereby. . . . Do you not remember being told that the Town Hall 'at home' was the centre of the mileage of the diverging roads, and being much impressed by this, the middle of the world, which should have been specially marked by a 'golden milestone'?"

In our mental geography, we recognize many centers to our orbits, the places where we were born and grew up, and those where we live, work, shop, and go for entertainment or worship. Like street gangs, we set boundaries to our local areas and feel at home within them. As well as personal centers, our territories contain places that we think of as local world-centers: Lethaby's town hall, the church, the cross in the market square. Beyond these are our national and cultural centers where state rituals are enacted.

In London, for example, the traditional town center is at Hyde Park Corner, the spot to which the radiating lines of milestones are directed. Adjoining it is the Duke of Wellington's Apsley House, to which is attributed the address No. 1, London. A rival spot, once regarded as the center of the British Empire, is the Eros statue in Piccadilly Circus. The monument at Charing Cross is also held to be London's center, though London tourist guides today say that everything is centered on the equestrian statue of Charles I in Trafalgar Square, from which all distances to London are measured.

In former times, the city center was believed to have been marked by London Stone, a mysterious, insignificant-looking block that is now lodged behind a grating in Cannon Street. Antiquarians have seen it as the old Roman Terminus, the stone sacred to Jupiter, which stood at the center of every Roman city. Its position was where the main axis, the *cardo maximus* running north–south, crossed the east–west line of the *decumanus*. It replicated the "golden milestone" within the Forum at Rome that marked the center of the Roman Empire.

The reputation of London Stone as the actual center, and also the mystical essence, of London is implied by an incident during the Cade Rebellion of 1450. At the head of his Kentish peasant army, Jack Cade, calling himself by the aristocratic name of Mortimer, entered the city, put the king to flight, and beheaded those of his advisers who were thought to be corrupt. The first thing he did upon riding into London was to smite London Stone with his sword, crying, "Now is Mortimer lord of this city!" So it was chronicled by Holinshed. Having done what was formally required of a conqueror, Cade seemed at a loss to know how to proceed further. In a few days, his rebellion petered out and he was dead.

Like every individual, every nation regards itself as occupying the world-center and being somehow distinguished above all other peoples. This perception can be the cause of egotism, and in modern times it has been absurdly and disastrously literalized in pseudoscientific theories about racial supremacy. Yet, as the anthropologists again witness, it is a universal perception and therefore natural, normal, and certainly ineradicable. Moreover, every nation and tribe has the inner knowledge, often expressed in its mythology, of being the original people and more truly human than anyone else. The proof of this, in every traditional society, is provided by a rock or pillar within the national sanctuary that is known to be the generation center of mankind and the spot where the pole of the universe penetrates the earth.

Another proof of centrality is that, at noon at the summer solstice, the sun stands right above the central pillar, which therefore casts no shadow. Such shadowless pillars were claimed in China, which boasted of being the Middle Kingdom; in India; and in other countries. Jerusalem was shown to be the world-center on the evidence of a lance without a midday shadow, and in Egypt a well at Syene, entirely illuminated by the solstitial sun at noon, was the legendary inspiration for Eratosthenes' feat of measuring the Earth's circumference.

It did not concern those who revered a national world-center that other such centers were revered by other nations. That was their business. Their own responsibility was to uphold their own culture and the sacred spot from which it was born. With their whole society focused on that spot, they had no attention to spare for the claims of other peoples, and no cause to envy them. Humanity can accept an infinity of world-centers without diminishing the unique qualities of any particular one. Thus, fashionable Londoners, to whom Sloane Square is the center of the universe, have no quarrel with the Muslims who locate it at Mecca.

Contemplating the Navel of the Earth

The center of the human body, halfway up and halfway down its front, is the navel. For this reason, and because it was once attached by the umbilical cord to our maternal source of life and nourishment, the navel provides an image of the notional world-center, the spot on the Earth's surface through which runs the universal pole. Both types of center, of the human and the terrestrial body, are similarly named: in Greek, *omphalos,* or in Latin, *umbilicus.*

Every religion has its world-center, with associated legends of being the first created spot on earth, the birthplace of humanity and the gateway to the two opposite realms or states of existence, the heavenly and the subterranean. In preindustrial times, the central point of each national and tribal territory was marked by a symbol of the polar shaft, and the omphalos stone in every town and village was also a cosmological center.

The perception behind this was that one's country and all its subdivisions, down to the village and the individual household, were small-scale, imperfect, but total reflections of the universe. Each part was an image of the whole, and vice versa. This perception is illustrated for us today by hologram images and the fractal patterns developed on computer screens. In these, one beholds chaos, or arbitrariness, interplaying with its opposite principle, order, which structures things similarly on every level of scale, until the two rivals disappear toward infinity, their contest never perceptibly resolved.

Traditional cosmologies describe a centered universe in which the principle of order is ultimately paramount. Their social product is a cosmologically ordered form of civilization whose central symbol is the world-pole penetrating the earth. A more familiar version is the shaft and bowl of a spindle, and mystically it is represented by the lance and grail vessel. Phallic and sexual connotations are certainly implied in these symbols, but they are by no means their primary references, as modern empirical speculators have been inclined to suppose.

As the locus of divine law, the cosmic pole is the most powerful symbol of authority and is regarded as the only legitimate source of human laws. Its many images include the scepter, the measuring rod, the king post, and the central pillar. Kings and chiefs are installed upon the local world-center rock, which empowers their rule, and when the rightful lawgiver pronounces from it, his words have the same unchallengeable force as if the rock itself had spoken.

Authority comes from the upward or, on a flat surface, the northern extension of the cosmic axis. This is its solar level and one of its two primary aspects. In its other aspect, the pole runs southward or down into the earth, into the lunar or night world of nature. From there comes the opposite principle to authority, the principle that subverts man-made order. Authority at the world-center is upheld by the omphalos rock, which retains the heat of the sun, while the lunar principle is active in the waters that rise beneath the rock, drawn by the moon and corresponding to the dimension of the mind below consciousness. In the same precinct as the world-center rock is a well, cave, or cleft in the earth—a therapeutic, oracular, and giving access to the underworld.

In Scandinavian and other mythologies, the world-axis is represented as the trunk of a great tree. Its branches reach to the heavens, its roots go down to the abyss, and its central section, where the trunk goes into and out of the earth, is our present plane of existence. When we discover that center, as a people or within our own selves, we can draw on divine guidance from above and imaginative inspiration from below the Earth's surface. In that situation, personally, geographically, and symbolically centered, one is at the hub of the universe and perfectly balanced to receive its full range of influences. Anyone who is thus centered is impelled toward justice, whether in self-rule or political government. Such a person is, in the esoteric sense only, King of the World, that mystical figure whose kingdom can be founded in the heart of any individual. As the reflection of God on earth, he is fair, merciful, and all-knowing, the philosopher-king of Platonic idealism. He is the complete, perfected image of oneself.

At the center of the Christian world is Golgotha, founded upon Adam's skull, the ancient rock on which Jesus was crucified. It is now built into the Jerusalem Church of the Holy Sepulchre, where its summit is kissed by pilgrims. Also kissed is a world-center pillar in the same church, erected and displayed by Greek priests. Nearby is the center of the Jews' world, the Rock of Foundation on the Temple Mount. Once it was enclosed by the gold-lined walls of the Holy of Holies in Solomon's Temple. Its legends claim it as the earth's navel, the first solid thing that God made and the center point of his creation. It is also known as the stopper, set above the crevice into which the last of Noah's flood subsided, with the purpose of holding down the waters forever.

Yet nothing in the material world is forever. On this and other rocks, great systems of law and religion have been founded, and the rock has sustained them over thousands of years. It is recognized, however, in the legend of the Rock of Foundation, that one day, sooner or later, the waters will rise again, dislodge the stopper, and wipe out all that has been built on and around it.

The destruction of a world-center by flood, fire, or other methods means the end of a whole world—which, if it is our world, we are inclined to identify with the world as a whole. There are many accounts of families, tribes, and whole nations dissolving upon the loss of their emblematic world-poles. An ancient family who lived by their pole were the MacDuffies, hereditary lords of the small

Hebridean island, Colonsay. Their talisman was a staff let into a hole in a stone base. The fortune of the MacDuffies, even their very existence, depended on it, and when it was stolen or somehow disappeared in 1539, the last chief of the MacDuffies died, and the lineage was broken.

Sir Baldwin Spencer and F. J. Gillen in *The Arunta* tell of an Australian tribe, the Achilpa, who were so attached to their emblematic polar axis, made for them by their divine ancestor from the trunk of a gum tree, that they carried it around with them on their migrations. It acted like a giant divining rod, showing by the way it bent the direction they should travel. When by accident the pole was broken, the tribe lost their focus and became disorientated. They wandered around aimlessly for a time, before lying down together and awaiting death.

This seems rather an extreme reaction, but the story is accepted by Mircea Eliade, who, in *The Sacred and the Profane,* gives other instances of devotion to the symbol of the cosmic pole. With the loss of their pole, he explains, the Achilpa lost contact with the ancestral spirits, forgot the meaning of their lives and landscape, and were plunged into chaos. He states, "Once contact with the transcendent is lost, existence in the world ceases to be possible—and the Achilpa let themselves die."

If this story is true (and anthropologists are as likely as anyone else to misunderstand just what is going on around them), the Achilpa are surely open to criticism for being too dependent on their worldview and its sacred symbol. There are many comparable accounts of tribes who have lapsed into apathy when their way of life and its symbols were destroyed by outsiders and of regiments who have given up the fight when their standard was captured. Yet we or our forebears have all had to make the transition from a traditional, centered universe to the worldview of aimlessness and relativism, which now prevails. Unlike the Achilpa, we have had a wide world in which to locate alternative centers to the structure of our lives and minds. This makes us seem less vulnerable to changes and accidents, such as the breaking of a pole. Yet modern life depends entirely upon an invisible pole, the international money system that every year grows more elaborate and more evidently beyond human control. If that pole were to snap, we would soon learn to admire the Achilpa for the dignified way in which they responded to the collapse of their own world order.

The Central Point of Paradise

An irrational but ever-popular notion, with deep mythological antecedents, is that the surface of the Earth has a central point. In all civilized times, people have known that the Earth is a globe, yet the image of a world-center mountain has attracted many educated writers and is accepted in all religions. As Mount Ararat was to Christian geographers, so is Mount Kailas in western Tibet to Hindus and Buddhists, awesomely regarded as the mountain at the center of the Earth.

The only spots on Earth that could reasonably be called its center are at the north and south poles, where the globe is conceptually penetrated by the universal axis. A recent book that touches upon this subject is Joscelyn Godwin's *Arktos.* Subtitled *The Polar Myth in Science, Symbolism, and Nazi Survival,* it summarizes the ideas of numerous writers, from pious philosophers to turbid fanatics, on the theory of human and cultural origins at the North Pole. Associated with this are certain beliefs, both ancient and modern, about the reality of a hollow Earth, the existence of a warm, paradisal Shangri-la behind the polar ice, and in the fanatical cases, Nordic racial superiority.

The world-center mountain, regarded as the transmitter of divine spirit and revelation, has the same mythological attributes as the poles and derives its symbolism from the concept of a world-axis. This does not imply literally that mankind descended from the polar regions. Yet on other levels, magnetic, spiritual, and symbolic, the poles of the

Earth have a considerable, though hidden influence on the human mind and constitution.

As the central mountain images the pole, so also does every central monument, every centered mind, and the pole-tree of every hut or tent. The pole is, of course, a magnet, and all its symbols are therefore generators of magnetic fields that extend their influence, however weakly, throughout the entire universe. Thus, every center can properly be seen as a world-center. Mystics and moralists have always said that every unit has its effect on every other, and modern physics has now fallen into line and proclaims the same truth.

The focus of anything or anywhere is also its essence. Thus, the design and symbolism of a center determines the character of its whole sphere of influence. Wherever the traditional worldview is upheld, every central spot is identified with the cosmological image of a world-pole that symbolizes divine law. The cosmology to which this image belongs is derived from the archetype of an ideal, divinely ordered, and centered universe where every element has its rightful place, both at the center and on the periphery of a fluctuating hierarchy, governed by harmony and proportion.

The ideal of a heavenly paradise is therefore taken as the model for the design of sanctuaries and whole countries, which then assume the character of a terrestrial paradise.

A temple or landscape that reflects the traditional image of paradise includes a number of essential features. A centrally placed stone, symbolically hermaphroditic, represents the omphalos receiving the universal pole. Below it lies the abyss, the entrance to which is seen nearby in a sacred well or an oracular cave. Around the stone is a sacred precinct, a microcosm of the whole territory, laid out as a formal model of paradise, with fountains, groves, shrines to the gods of the four quarters, and altars to the twelve winds.

The omphalos is the source of all goodness, symbolized by the four rivers of paradise that issue from it toward the four points of the compass. These may be identified with local springs and streams, and they are also represented diagrammatically by four highways extending at right angles from the central point. They divide the country into four main sections, and further subdivisions, into eight, twelve, and lesser units, are established by boundary marks. The land is apportioned fairly among all the tribes and families; local centers are founded as their places of festival and council, and each locality is dedicated to one of the twelve zodiacal gods, with shrines and feast days for the spirits of the countryside. The whole order of things is based on a formal, mathematically structured image of the cosmos, adapted as the pattern for a mythological landscape whose spiritual aspect is emphasized in the relationship between its natural and man-made features.

According to the evidence laid out in the following chapters, the first thing that was needed by those who created sacred landscapes was to locate the country's main axis, the preferably north–south line between its two extremities, passing through the center. It corresponded to the world-tree, the shaman's pole by which he ascends to the world of spirits, and all other symbols of the universal axis. It was a ritual path and an Earthly reflection of the Milky Way, which, says Eliade, is an image of the world-axis in the sky.

Guarding and overlooking the omphalos, generally to the north of it in the direction from which disruptive forces are traditionally supposed to emanate, is found a lone, conical mountain. Its mythological prototype is the mountain at the center of the world. The chief god of the pantheon resides there, presiding awesomely over the rituals in his sanctuary below.

The traditional sacred landscape, it seems, was laid out on three main dimensions of scale, with the central shrine, the sanctuary district, and the whole country each reflecting the same archetypal design. The object of this and how it was achieved are described in Plato's *Laws,* his picture of a society modeled on the formal world image of traditional cosmology.

Plato claimed that his ideal city-state was the best, most satisfying, most just, and most long-lasting form of society, allowing the greatest amount of happiness to the greatest possible number of its citizens. This state is strikingly similar to the old twelve-tribe federations, known as *amphictyonies* (dwellers around a central sanctuary), which existed around every notable religious center in archaic Greece. The best known of these institutions was the Pylaea, the council of the twelve neighboring tribes that guarded and administered the sacred Apollonian lands around Delphi and Mount Parnassus. Other such amphictyonies, throughout and far beyond the ancient Greek world, are described in a previous book, written with Christine Rhone, *Twelve-Tribe Nations and the Science of Enchanting the Landscape.*

Before Plato's time (around 400 BC), the advance of civilization, with commerce, wealth, and militarism, had corrupted the old, rustic amphictyonies. Plato evidently wanted to restore them in their pure, pristine form, most closely resembling their ideal, cosmological foundation plan.

Plato's *Laws,* as well as his *Timaeus* and other works, is therefore a prime source for investigators of ancient, cosmologically ordered societies and their symbolic landscapes. His city-state, in Book V of the *Laws* was laid out as an astrological chart of the heavens. In the middle of the capital was the citadel and omphalos, from which twelve radial lines were drawn, dividing the land and people into twelve tribes, and each section was placed under one of the twelve zodiacal gods. Each tribe had its own regional focus, which imitated the national capital and was also centrally placed. The whole scheme was governed by a cosmological number code. Plato did not openly exhibit it, but represented it by the number 5040. This number, divisible by all the base numbers from 1 to 10, allows the maximum number of subdivisions down to the smallest center, the household hearth. It is also a key number in the cosmological code, described in the final chapter, which provided the ground plan for ritually ordered, twelve-tribe societies throughout the world.

Surveyors and Geomancers

Plato, in the *Laws,* emphasizes that the state citadel must be placed "as nearly as possible in the very centre of the country." He does not say how the central spot is to be defined, nor how it is to be located, but such matters were always attended to by a body of specialists within the priesthood. Mystical methods of finding the correct site for temples and ritual centers were known to these specialists in every old religious system. In Western Christendom, they seem to have died out with the Middle Ages, and modern scholars have paid so little attention to their science that we do not even have an agreed upon name for it. Modern investigators of symbolic landscapes have filled this gap, not to everyone's satisfaction, by calling it geomancy—the art of divination applied to the earth. Its practitioners in ancient Rome belonged to the College of Augurs and were responsible for choosing the correct site and foundation date for temples and public buildings. Romulus, the founder of Rome, was said to have been the first augur. The Greek augurs were the Oionistai; their art of divination by the flight of birds was commemorated by the two gold eagles that stood in effigy upon the omphalos stone at Delphi.

Augurs or geomancers still have their place in the old Eastern religions and in traditional societies everywhere, though modern secularization now limits their functions. Like the *feng-shui* specialists of China, who were formerly state officials under the Board of Rites, geomancers today work mainly for private clients, advising on the most favorable sites and designs for houses, shops, and offices.

Nothing directly is known about the people who first established the symbolic centers of ancient countries. Analogy suggests that they were priestly diviners who were trained, as Caesar says of the Druids, in astronomy, astrology, geodesy, and land measurement. They are also the traditional subjects of geomancy, together with number, cosmology, and the subtle arts of aesthetics and divination. Despite Caesar's hint, accurate surveying is not generally attributed to the ancient priesthoods. Legends of omphalos foundations usually describe some feat of divination, such as the releasing of two eagles from opposite ends of the earth and their meeting at Delphi. Yet the evidence of the examples given in this book indicates that land surveying is a very ancient skill. Much has been discovered in recent years about the advanced knowledge of preliterate astronomers. Astronomy is closely associated with land measurement, and no doubt the two sciences have long flourished together. We should not therefore be surprised to find that ancient surveying and geodesy were, like ancient astronomy, scientifically developed.

It may seem incongruous to link astronomy and surveying, which we now regard as more or less exact sciences, with divination through signs in nature. Yet the omphalos legends tell of divination, rather than of someone actually measuring something. In this subject, we are dealing with a priestly science that hid its mechanical mysteries beneath a cloak of myth and allegory. We hear of the two eagles meeting, of someone who shot an arrow, of someone else who killed a serpent, and of a stone that fell from heaven. They provide a far more interesting, compelling, and authoritative reason for the siting of the omphalos at a particular spot than the mundane information that the priests measured it out.

At the same time, the location of the symbolic center is not simply a matter of measurement. Divination has an important part in it, for, as Plato tells his colonists, the site of the symbolic center must have certain physical and spiritual qualities that befit it as the national omphalos. It should be favorably influenced by all its elements—its winds, sunshine, soil, and water. Above all, says Plato, the spot must be spiritually favorable. That is a quality that only the augur or geomancer can divine. How well they succeeded can be judged through some of the following examples of symbolic centers, where geographical accuracy is combined with the practical requirements for an assembly and with a spiritually, symbolically appropriate landscape setting.

Open-Air Government

In 1880, Sir George Laurence Gomme, the pioneer folklorist, published his *Primitive Folk-Moots.* Subtitled *Open-Air Assemblies in Britain,* it was packed with curious items of history and antiquarian lore in evidence of Gomme's thesis, that in former times and often until quite recently, all business of justice and law making was conducted in the open air, in popular assemblies at certain customary spots. Despite the cajoling of nobles and clergymen, covered courts were long resisted. People said that at a meeting within a building, one could easily be bewitched.

Under the Anglo-Saxon system, the Witenagemot (meeting of wise men) or national parliament was accessible to all free citizens and included deputies from the shire moots. These in turn were drawn from the hundred moots, and these from the local folkmoots, the members of which were elected by their immediate neighbors. Rank and privilege certainly had their say, and franchise was not universal, but confined to freemen; yet as a type of democracy this arrangement had certain qualities that the modern version lacks. At least everyone knew personally the candidate they were voting for.

Corresponding to the English folkmoots and manor courts were the Scandinavian Things, or Tings, beginning with the *husthing,* which discussed the affairs of a hamlet or farmstead. From this humble institution comes our word "hustings," while the word "meeting" comes from *mote-thing,* an assembly on a mound. There were village Things, regional and provincial Things, and at midsummer everyone came together around the national omphalos for the high point of the year, the Al-thing.

In old English, Celtic, Nordic, and Germanic societies—and no doubt everywhere else in the premodern world—meetings and meeting places abounded. Apart from the festivals that followed the religious calendar and were held at fixed times and places, there were many other assemblies that took place when the need arose, for legal purposes or in times of war. Kings, chiefs, priests, and judges all required their own courts or ritual centers, and every craft and trade had its regular place of convention.

All these meetings were held in the open air. This was the Druids' practice, and one of their sayings was often quoted by those in later times who objected to indoor assemblies: that every public meeting, for whatever purpose, should always be held "under the eye of the sun."

Odin, chief god in the Norse pantheon, upheld the same rule, for every Thing imitated the open plain, high up in the world-tree, where Odin sat at the central shaft, enthroned amid his twelve divine counselors.

The twelve gods of every structured religion come from the pagan, solar way of dividing the zodiac, the calendar, and everything else into units of twelve, and from that also has come the pattern of twelve heroes, knights, berserkers, judges, witches, or counselors that typifies the mythology and institutions of the Bronze Age. Every Thing district was divided into four and then into twelve main units, and the judges or officials at a Thing always numbered twelve, like a modern jury, or a multiple thereof.

The traditional places of assembly were marked in all kinds of ways—by rocks, pillars, trees, springs, mounds, crossroads, and other features. Meetings were held in dales, on hilltops, or on islets in lakes and rivers. Stone circles, ancient earthworks, and menhirs were sometimes the focus, and some meeting places were distinguished by nothing more than the legend that they had been used "from time immemorial."

Most of these old assemblies have long been forgotten, but their memory is often retained in the traditional names of their centers and districts. All over England are found hills named Moot or Mote, tumuli named Law or Low, Shire or County oaks, Hundred thorns, and names including Gorse or Gorsey (the Welsh *gorsedd*), Dom or Doom (law), and Rad (the Anglo-Saxon *raed,* or council). English place-names, commemorating the site of a Thing in times of Viking rule, include Thingwall village near Liverpool, Thingwall parish in Cheshire, Tingley or Ting-law near Leeds, Tinwell in Rutland, Tingrith in Bedfordshire, and the hundred (a country subdivision) of Thingoe in Suffolk. Scottish examples include the town of Dingwall, Tinwald Hill in Dumfriesshire, and Thingswa near Thurso, Caithness.

Thing sites were laid out in many different ways, probably in accordance with their various functions. Law courts were typically held on natural or artificial mounds commanding a wide view of their district. At the center was a tree, stone, or pit, or a combination of these, and the periphery was defined by one or more rings of stones or earth. The first formality consisted of "fencing" the court, that is, drawing and marking its boundary. Inside the fence was the hallowed ground, where rules of conduct were prescribed by law and religion.

The climax to the year's round of festivals and law meetings was the grand convention from all the local districts at the central Gemor, or Al-thing. Its forms and functions were the same as those of the regional Things, but on a more elaborate scale. These assemblies had one basic purpose, to uphold standards in all things legal, cultural, and physical. The laws were proclaimed publicly in the open air; matters of inheritance, land rights, and lawsuits between neighbors were settled locally, while serious crimes and disputes between districts were referred to higher courts.

Cultural standards were maintained by bardic and musical competitions; there were athletic contests, trials of craftsmanship and stock breeding, and displays representing every aspect of social life. Everyone who could possibly do so attended the Al-thing. Tents and booths were set up around the center, and for a week or so people did their own business, arranging deals and marriages and socializing at fairs and parties.

In pagan times, every law gathering was held on the feast day and at the sanctuary of a certain god, whose authority was assumed by the judges and rulers installed there. That same authority maintained the principles of free expression, protecting the rights of anyone who spoke within the sacred enclosure. The origins of this institution have been traced back to the earliest times: when groups of tribal nomads sat together in discussion at the end of a day's journey, when they listened to storytellers and the guidance of their shamans, when they met and took counsel with other wanderers, when they came together for midsummer at the tribal sanctuary. These events took place in a regular yearly sequence at particular spots around the country, and this pattern has continued in the holding of assizes, when judges make a circuit of the provincial courts before presiding at the national law center.

Open-air assemblies in historical times were often held at stone circles and other megalithic sites thousands of years old. In some cases, the tradition was probably as old as the monument itself, hinting at an original purpose of these ancient sites as the local fonts of law and religion. An example is the beautiful, secluded Boscawen-un stone circle in west Cornwall, referred to in the old *Welsh Triads* as a *gorsedd*, or meeting place of bardic lawgivers. Its nineteen erect stones seem to have been carefully chosen to represent a range of symbols, as if for an assembly from different clans or districts, and it provides the focus for many of the standing stones in the surrounding country, which are precisely aligned on it. In King's *Munimenta Antiqua*, it is said that Boscawen-un was a place where kings were elected. Other stone circles, the Rollright stones in Oxfordshire and the Derbyshire circle, Nine Ladies, have similar legends.

From these centers, the land was measured out and given fixed borders. One of the traditional ruler's main duties was to uphold the divisions and landmarks, and that was symbolized by the measuring rod he received at the ceremony of installation. By virtue of this rod, he was enabled to mete out justice. Every Celtic chief bore such a rod. Its polar symbolism was emphasized by its length, which if graded by the ancient geodetic units, was a specific fraction of the Earth's axis. The same rod was applied to the ruler's physical frame as a test of

how he "measured up" to his position. A feature of Celtic installation sites is a footprint, carved into the upper surface of a rock, that
fits the foot of every rightful king, as the slipper fitted Cinderella's.
An indentation, known locally as a giant's footprint, can be seen in a
rocky outcrop, possibly the original place of installation, just above
the circle at Boscawen-un.

The powers of ancient kings, chiefs, priests, and lawgivers were
not of human origin but were derived and borrowed from the symbolic center. This was also regarded as the birthplace of the tribe, so
it belonged to the people as a whole rather than to any ruler they
might elect. Once chosen, the king was irradiated with the misti-
cal power of the center and became the agent and interpreter of its
influence. Installed upon the local world-center rock, at the point of
mediation between the law of heaven and the will of the people, he
surveyed the cosmologically ordered divisions of his realm. Its ritual
boundaries, defining the spiritual, astrological limits of each section,
may have been marked by the straight alignments of stone pillars like
those that converge on Boscawen-un and other stone circles.

It was a glorious thing to be installed at the center as king of the
world, and it must have felt glorious to the people that they possessed
such a prodigy. Yet they, like the ruler, demanded high standards. If
the king was just and noble-minded, as well as strong and virile, the
country prospered, enemies were defeated, the weather was favorable,
good luck prevailed, and the rhythm of life went harmoniously. If he
was flawed, the order of nature was upset, and the social order with
it. If his symbolic marriage with the native goddess showed signs of
going wrong and the country became fruitless and dissatisfied, the
people who chose the king would summarily dismiss him, sometimes
fatally, upon the authority of their rock.

Something of the mystical atmosphere from their early days has
clung to the ancient assembly places, preserving their sanctity along
with many of their quaint archaic customs. One of Gomme's examples
was the Free Court of Corbey in Saxony. Its procedures, he found,

were essentially the same as in pagan times, when it was directed by
the priests of Eresburg. The court's main business was to adminis-
ter the common lands of the district wherein it was centered. There
were sixteen lifelong members, presided over by a *graff* who occupied
the king's seat in the middle of a plot of land measuring sixteen by
sixteen feet. The judges sat four to each side of this plot, and before
they began their work, they each threw a handful of ashes, a coal, and
a tile into a pit dug within it. If these tokens could not subsequently
be found, all judgments given at that session were invalidated. It was
essential that the court be held "beneath the sky and by the light of
the sun."

With the declamation of age-old verses, the court began by assay-
ing the measuring wands used for land surveying. They were ceremonially tested against the length of the graff's right foot and with the
foot of each judge in turn. The plot around the king's seat was then
measured with these wands, and only when it was confirmed as a true
sixteen-foot square could proceedings begin.

There were many similar institutions in old Saxony, survivors of
the pagan system that prevailed there until 772, when Charlemagne
broke it at one stroke, cutting down the Irminsul, the central pole
representing the axis and world-tree within the national sanctuary at
Eresburg. This, said a ninth-century writer (quoted in Eliade's *The
Sacred and the Profane*), was "the pillar of the universe which as it
were, supports all things." The destruction of their Irminsul, it seems,
had much the same effect on the pagan Saxons as the breaking of
their pole on the aforementioned Achilpa tribe.

Modern Centers: America, Australia

In a cow pasture two miles northwest of Lebanon, Kansas, at a point
of latitude 39° 50' N, longitude 98° 35' W, stands a limestone shaft
with a flagpole flying the Stars and Stripes. It marks the geographical
center of the forty-eight (not counting Alaska and Hawaii) United

Figure 1. The monument that marks the geographical center of the United States at Lebanon, Kansas.

States of America. Likewise in Australia, the national geographers have taken counsel and have caused a similar monument to be erected on an unremarkable spot in the bush, which they calculated to be the omphalos of the Australian continent.

These landmarks serve no practical purpose, but appeal to the curious-minded, or to the curious part of everyone's mind. They are monuments to our instinctive, everlasting perception that every being, even a large, self-confident modern nation, needs to affirm its own identity by finding its own center.

Figure 2. The official, geographical center of South America in western Brazil, visited by English artist Keith Payne.

In geographical institutions today, there are specialists known as centrographers, whose business it is to locate centers. For the most part, they look for the center of a given mass or type of population. This is called the median center, defined as "the place where the sum of the distances to each person is a minimum." It is found by drawing a straight line (strictly speaking, a great circle) across the map so as to divide the group in question into two equal parts. The group is then again divided into two by a line at an angle to the first, and the median center is where the two lines cross.

To find the geographical center of a country, some centrographers proceed in imitation of Sir Charles Arden-Close, whose method of establishing the center of England is described in detail in chapter 5. Others have different ways of going about it. The American geographers who discovered the midpoint of the United States used the "center of gravity" approach. They pasted the map of America on a board, cut out the relevant area, and found its point of balance on a vertical pivot. As stated in a pamphlet published by the U.S. Department of Commerce, "What might be called the geographic center is that point at which the map will balance.

The geographers' map balancing produced only an approximate result. Kansas citizens had always known themselves to be centrally placed in the United States, and several places promoted themselves as the actual focus. Local rivals to Lebanon included Junction City, Smith Center, and Fort Riley. To establish their claim, the people of Lebanon formed the neatly named Hub Club. They commissioned a firm of Kansas engineers to narrow the range of possible center sites, and in 1939 they acquired for $50 a half-acre plot in the "central area." A Lebanon builder used local stone to construct the marker, a bronze plaque was attached to it, recording its meaning and the sponsorship of the Hub Club, and a lady living nearby volunteered to raise and lower the U.S. flag on the flagpole every morning and night. The monument has become a popular success; many people go there each year, sign the visitors' book, and enjoy the feeling of being at the very center of America.

The Lebanon center was challenged in 1959 when Alaska and Hawaii were admitted to the Union. Finding the new center required another calculation, which was carried out, oddly enough, by members of the National Ocean Survey. This is how they defined their task:

> The geographical center of the combination of Alaska and the forty-eight conterminous states is considered to be on the great circle connecting their geographic centers at a point where the two areas would "balance"; i.e., considering each having a weight, proportional to its area, concentrated at the corresponding geographic center.

Including Alaska, the United States' center was found to be about eleven miles west of Castle Rock, Butte County, South Dakota. The admission of Hawaii caused the center to move six miles further west. These reckonings, says the National Ocean Survey modestly, are accurate to within about ten miles in any direction.

In 1988, during the bicentennial celebrations, the Royal Geographical Society of Australia (RGSA) decided to place a monument at the center of the Australian mainland. The necessary calculations were performed by centrographers at the Queensland Department of Geographic Information, and on September 10, a ceremonial procession, the Centre Safari, set out from Brisbane to identify the spot.

The method used by the Queensland centrographers was to inform a computer of the coordinates of 24,417 coastal points, from which they obtained two great circles, each dividing the area of the country into two equal halves. The center point was where the two lines intersected. It turned out to be in Northern Territory, about fifty miles north of the border with South Australia, at latitude 25° 36' 36.4" S, longitude 134° 21' 17.3" E.

The Centre Safari lasted for three weeks. The eighty-five RGSA members from Queensland, with another forty-six from South Australia, traveled by coach and four-wheel-drive vehicles toward the center point, which they discovered in a patch of scrub on Lilla Creek Station. There they erected the center monument, a replica of the flagpole on Parliament House in Canberra. Its ceremonial unveiling was attended by some two hundred people, including eminent geographers and representatives of the local Aborigines.

The leader of the safari, Dr. L. J. Isdale, president of Queensland's RGSA branch, was surprised to find that he was by no means the first Australian to identify a national center. In the same district, there were already at least seven other claimants, including the Aboriginal world-center at Ayers Rock, Central Mount Stuart, and the town of Alice Springs. Previous geographers had set up a geodetic station nearby as the base point for the National Survey, and this had its supporters as the true center. Not everyone supported the Queenslanders' definition of the center. Centrographers of other states wanted to mark the median point, lying midway between the continental extremes of latitude and longitude, and some preferred the tidal center, the point most remote from tidal water. To avoid rancor, the Centre Safari was tactfully extended to include celebrations of all those points.

To justify all the ceremonial pageantry, Isdale hoped that it "succeeded in raising public awareness of the geography of inland Australia." This seems rather lame, when he might well have claimed that by putting up his pole in the desert he had performed the necessary ritual to establish the identity of Australia and its existence as a whole.

Principles of Symbolic Centrography

The sites of ancient ritual centers and national assemblies had certain features in common with geographical and median centers, as previously defined, but they were not the same thing and they were located by different methods. Through the study of ancient ritualized landscapes, where the position of the former sanctuary is still known, certain geographical principles behind their siting have been observed, and it has been possible to apply them to the rediscovery of national centers in countries where they have long been forgotten.

Every territory has a different and sometimes an awkwardly irregular shape, so in every case the location of the symbolic center involves a compromise. No one site could possess all the features that ideally characterize the omphalos, but the following principles were evidently consulted by the priestly geomancers who established the ritual centers of their various countries.

The first principle was to identify the main axis of the territory, the longest line that can be drawn between its two opposite extremities. Preferably, this should be the north–south axis, emphasizing the symbolism of a world-pole. As nearly as possible, it should bisect the land and the people into two equal halves.

The southernmost point of a country seems to be the most important. From there, the axis is drawn upward to the appropriate northern spot, imitating the growth of the world-tree from its roots. Ideally speaking, the symbolic center should be located on the main north–south axis, either halfway along it or at its intersection with a cross axis between the eastern and western extremities.

The site must also be spiritually and practically appropriate. It should be easily accessible from all quarters, suitable for large assemblies, and commandingly placed, with wide views across the landscape, particularly to the south, and the northern approach being sheltered by a guardian mountain. The ideal site is secluded and mystically potent, and flanked by hill ranges to the east and west, so that whoever sits there looking southward is naturally enthroned.

To find examples of such centers, it is easiest to examine island territories, whose boundaries are defined by nature. Almost all the examples studied in the following chapters are on islands, mostly in the British Isles with Celtic or Nordic cultures. Without further research, one cannot be sure how universal was this system of locating national sanctuaries and capitals on the country's main axis. As shown by the examples below from Egypt and Greece, it was certainly not confined to northern Europe. At the omphalos sites of ritualized societies around the world, similar traditions occur, implying that similar principles and methods were used by those who first located them.

Ancient Egypt and Greece

The subject of ancient ritual geography, involving the relative siting of national temples and oracle centers, has been studied by several modern writers. Most impressive is the evidence of ancient Egypt, a country of natural symmetry, with its polar axis entwined by the river Nile. Its geography is naturally receptive to symbolism, and the Egyptian cosmological religion set its mark over the entire country. With temples, obelisks, and geodetic pillars, the land of Egypt was laid out as a sanctuary of the gods, divided and measured in accordance with the priestly science of proportion.

In his formidable work on Egyptian measurements and land surveying, Livio Stecchini shows how carefully and accurately the ruling priesthood sited the main ritual centers, using degrees of latitude to locate geographically significant sites. From the rise of the Eleventh Dynasty in about 2160 BC, the holy city of Thebes, with its great temples of Luxor and Karnak, was the official center of Egypt. An omphalos stone marking the exact midpoint stood in the temple of Amon, the seat of the national oracle. It was significantly placed where the line of latitude 25° 42' 51" N (two-sevenths of the distance from the equator to the pole) crosses the Nile and intersects with the meridian 32° 38' E, which Stecchini identifies as one of three meridian lines that define the width of the Nile delta and extend southward to form the ritual boundaries of sacred Egypt.

Akhenaten, the revolutionary pharaoh, came to power in 1388 BC, and during his thirty-year reign, he overturned the entire political and religious order of old Egypt, including the system of geomancy and ritual geography based on Thebes. The ancient city was abandoned, and all its institutions and powers were transferred to a new capital, Akhtaten, where a new state god was proclaimed—Aten, the power of the sun.

The magnificent city of Akhtaten was built over many square miles, in the course of a few years, on a site that had previously been almost uninhabited. It was a vast, urgent labor, and the necessity for it has been a puzzle to historians ever since. Evidently the young Pharaoh was gripped by some new idea, acting upon him with the force of a revelation, which impelled him to undertake his radical enterprise. The key to his motive is the site where he insisted on building Akhtaten, a lonely, inaccessible spot with poor land and an unfavorable climate. Yet it possessed a unique quality, making it the only suitable site for the capital of Akhenaten's new Egypt. It happened to be on the pole of the country and exactly halfway along it,

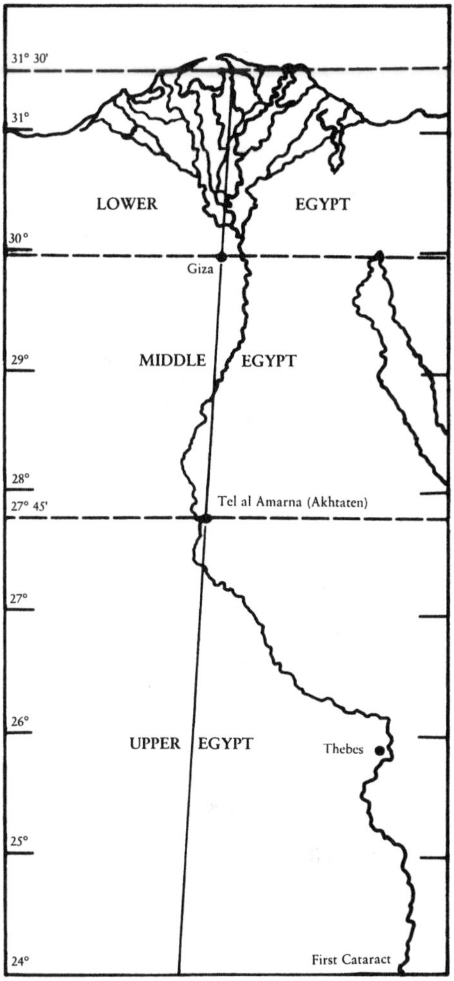

Figure 3. Precisely midway between the formal northern and southern limits of ancient Egypt, at latitudes 31° 30' and 24°, respectively, on the central axis of the country, the solar Pharaoh Akhenaten founded his new capital. Its central position symbolized his ruling philosophy. The ruins of Akhtaten are near the modern settlement at Tel al Amarna.

where the line from the northernmost point of Egypt, at latitude 31° 30' N, crosses the Nile midway on its course to the southern border at latitude 24°.

Proof of Akhtaten's geographical significance was found by Stecchini in rock inscriptions and geodetic markers around the old city, describing foundation rituals and recording long-distance measurements. The site, it appears, had to fulfill two simple conditions, that it should be on the Nile and midway between the northern and southern limits of the kingdom.

This indicates the nature of Akhenaten's revelation. Like many rulers and their priests before and after him, he was initiated into the secrets of the mystical science whose main symbol is the universal pole. With his throne established at the center of the world, beside the axis pole from which all distances were measured, Akhenaten assumed the powers of an almighty, divinely appointed sovereign, personifying both the land of Egypt below and its ruler, Aten, the god above. In all the records of Akhenaten, the word constantly associated with his rule is *maet,* meaning truth, justice, and the perfect order of the cosmos. The same principle, *li,* was upheld by the solar emperors of old China. Akhenaten's style of rule was that of sacred kings throughout history. Through the arts and ritual of priestcraft, he made himself a channel for maet, the law of heaven, which, when brought to govern human affairs, transforms the world and makes it an earthly paradise.

Akhenaten's attempt to establish maet and sacred rule throughout Egypt did not survive him. After his death, the old Theban priesthood regained control, his monuments were defaced, his capital fell into ruins, and his system of geomancy and ritual land measurement was abandoned.

Many centuries later another Thebes, the famous Greek city in Boeotia, produced a leader who also founded a capital city on the symbolic pole of a country. In 370 BC, the Theban commander, Epaminondas, defeated the Spartans, and in order to perpetuate his advantage, built an enormous, fortified city, confidently named Megalopolis, meaning "Great City," in the middle of Peloponnesus. It was different in scale from the tribal city-states of contemporary Greece, a densely populated, cosmopolitan center with magnificent temples and public buildings, opulent villas, and extensive suburbs. For well over a hundred years, it succeeded in its purpose of overawing the Spartans, but eventually it dwindled away into insignificance.

Epaminondas was of a noble but impoverished family, and his great advantage in life came from his father's hospitality to an exiled

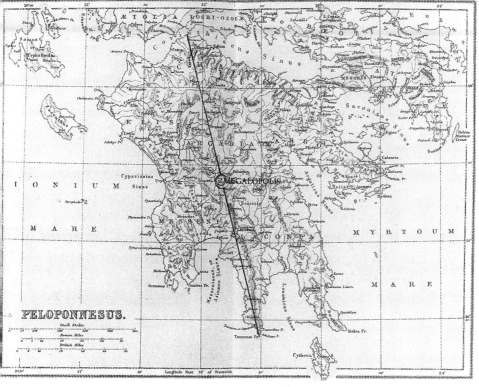

Figure 4. Near the midpoint of the main north–south axis of Peloponnesus, Epaminondas founded Megalopolis (Great City) in the fourth century BC.

Pythagorean philosopher, who became his tutor. The Pythagoreans and the professors of Plato's Academy concentrated their educational efforts on young men who were likely to become rulers. They taught the techniques of statecraft, which were not secret but openly displayed in Plato's *Laws*. The founder of a state is therein instructed to place his capital, as near as possible, in the center of the country. Ideally, it should be halfway along the north–south axis. Epaminondas had evidently learned that lesson, for when he chose the site for Megalopolis he made it, as near as was practical, lie at the halfway point on the polar axis of Peloponnesus, on the direct line between its northernmost and southernmost extremities.

Mediolanum, the Center of Gaul

Every Celtic community, tribe, and national federation of tribes had its sacred assembly place of law and justice. They were centrally placed at the midpoint of their territories, and under Roman influence, the name given to the more important centers was Mediolanum. The word has a double meaning, implying physically the center of a plain and symbolically the center of paradise. About sixty Mediolanum names are known, mostly in Gaul. The prototype was Mediolanum, the modern Milan, in Cisalpine Gaul, northern Italy.

Several French villages dispute with each other about the right to be called the center of France. Their nearest city, Bourges, takes its name from the Celtic tribe that occupied this central district, the Bituriges. Experts derive their name from the prefix *bitu,* meaning both the world and time, and *riges,* the plural of *rix* or *ri,* the Celtic king. The Bituriges were therefore the people of the central province, ruled directly by the mortal representative of the king of the world, lord of the ages. These titles were assumed by the Celtic high king, enthroned at the sacred center of his country and people, the central country and the central people of the whole world.

The Mediolanum that has most the support as the central town of France is Châteaumeillant (Middle Castle) in the land of the Bituriges. Its position justifies its name, for it stands very near the halfway point on the main north–south axis of France, the line from the northernmost point at the Belgian border, passing through Paris to the southern border with Spain.

Another centrally situated place of Celtic assembly, ritual, and government, referred to in Caesar's *Gallic War,* was in the tribal land of the Carnutes at Chartres. "The Druids at a certain time of the year meet within the borders of the Carnutes, whose territory is reckoned to be the centre of all Gaul, and sit in conclave at a consecrated spot. Assembled there from all quarters are those who have disputes, and they all obey the Druids' judgments and decisions."

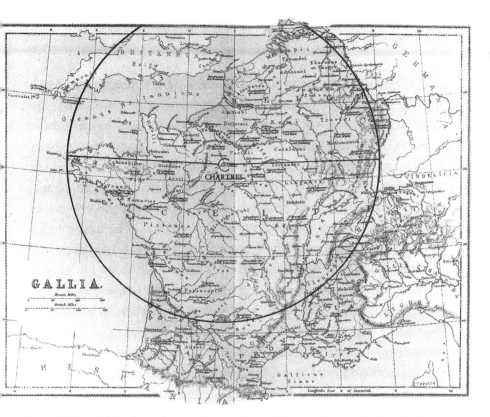

Figure 5. The Celtic place of national assembly, at Chartres in the tribal lands of the Carnutes, was centrally placed within the Celtic realm, equidistant from its western and eastern extremities at the tip of Brittany and the mouth of the Rhine. A circle through those points, centered on Chartres, includes the whole of Celtic Gaul, omitting the Roman provinces in the south.

Caesar goes on to say that Druidry first arose in Britain and from there was introduced into Gaul. It came, in other words, from the north, the land nearest to the pole, and in that Hyperborean region its deepest mysteries were preserved. "Those who would study the subject [the Druidic arts] most thoroughly still travel to Britain to learn it." All too briefly, Caesar then describes the subjects taught in the Druidic colleges. "They discuss and teach youths about the heavenly bodies and their motions, the dimensions of the world and of countries, natural science and the powers of the immortal gods."

The remarkable centrality of Chartres has previously attracted comment. In the first volume of *The Circle and the Cross,* A. Hadrian Allcroft is erudite and perceptive on the subject of Things, moots, and world-centers. In some cases, he suspected a geographical factor in their central locations. Stonehenge, he noticed, "is all but equi-distant from Land's End, from Holyhead, and from the north-east extremity of the Norfolk coast," concluding that "this can hardly be altogether a matter of accident." He suggested that Stonehenge was the national assembly place of the Belgic Britons.

Allcroft observed that Chartres, the reputed center of all Gaul, was indeed situated as nearly as possible at the midpoint of the Celtic territories, equidistant from their eastern and western limits—the far end of Brittany and the river Rhine. A circle with its center on Chartres—where tradition locates the ancient place of assembly on the site of the cathedral—neatly defines the Gallia of Caesar's time, excluding the Roman provinces in the south of France, including the Belgic settlements in southern England, and denoting the natural boundary at the mouth of the Rhine.

2

THE NORTHERN ISLES

Picts and Vikings

Judging by traditions and place-names, there were numerous Thing places throughout the northern, formerly Norwegian, islands of Orkney and Shetland. Only a few of their sites are precisely known, but the most wonderful example still exists, the former Shetland Al-thing. Certain of its features, notably its position at the true symbolic center, arouse intriguing speculations about its date, the means of its location, and the science of the people who first established it.

The dozen or so inhabited isles of Shetland, and many others that are depopulated, lie nearer to Oslo and Reykjavik than to London and derive their traditions from a long period of Viking rule, beginning in the seventh or eighth century. In 1469, King Christian I of Denmark, Norway, and Sweden, whose daughter was marrying the king of Scotland, pledged the islands as security for her dowry, which he never paid. Despite repeated efforts by the Danes to redeem the pledge, Shetland was subsequently ruled from Edinburgh and, after the Act of Union, from London. The present population of Shetland is about 23,000, about half of whom live in the capital, Lerwick, on the largest island, Mainland.

The pre-Norse occupants of Shetland were the mysterious people called Picts, who were probably the aboriginal descendants of the first farmers and megalith builders, and of the nomadic hunters who preceded them. Judging by their remarkable sculptured stones, relics, and numerous farmsteads, they were cultured and populous. There is evidence that, in a country now almost treeless, they had large, wooden ceremonial halls. During the Iron Age, from about 700 BC, they seem to have grown more defensive and warlike, perhaps in response to pressure from Irish and Scandinavian raiders. At strong points in their northern Scottish and island territories, they built magnificent structures called *brochs*—tall, many-story, drystone towers, curving inward from the base rather like a bottle kiln and capable of lodging about a hundred people. Around them were settlements of thatched stone huts enclosed within a rampart. At least seventy-five brochs have been recognized in Shetland, sometimes on remote, long-uninhabited islands. There is a greater density and there are finer examples of them here than anywhere else, and it has been suggested that the broch was an original product of the Shetland genius.

The Pictish farmlands in Shetland were carefully surveyed and apportioned out in field systems with fixed boundaries. Larger tribal or clan borders were settled permanently by broad stone walls that sometimes ran for miles across whole islands. An impressive example is the Finnigord, which divides the island of Fetlar into two halves. Like other mighty works of the ancients, it was attributed in Norse times to the Finns, a phantom race with magical powers who are much recorded in Shetland folklore. Up to the eighteenth century, the sanctity of the old divisions and boundaries was regularly reaffirmed at the ceremony of "riding the hagri," where the bounds were beaten, as also were the young lads, in order to impress their memories with the lines and landmarks.

The Picts resisted Christianity long after it was introduced into Scotland, but in the days of the Celtic Church, Christians and pagans were remarkably tolerant of each other; by at least the fifth century, Irish monks were well established in Shetland, and most of the Pictish tribes were probably converted. Religion in those days was not so much an individual as a social matter. Local chiefs were persuaded by missionaries of the practical advantages that Christianity would bring their people, such as magical superiority and victory in battle, and whole tribes were converted together.

Christianity did little to change the existing social order. As in pagan times, every small community had its sanctuary, replacing the previous Druidic enclosure but normally on the same spot. On it, the Christians either built a simple chapel or adapted the old pagan sanctum. They were not like modern churches, places of public worship, but were reserved for the religious mysteries and the preservation of relics. Popular gatherings for ritual, justice, and other purposes were held as before in the open air, on a mound beside or near the chapel. A sacred well or spring was usually located nearby.

The Picts were widely distributed over all the inhabitable isles of Shetland, so there were many communities, chapels, and places of meeting. Their system of land divisions was probably maintained by the incoming Norse farmers, for it is difficult and unreasonable to move established, well-marked borders, upsetting the entire social and economic pattern. Norse lands were measured according to their value, by what they could produce in terms of wealth or serving men. An ounceland paid tax to the king of one ounce of silver a year, and was divided into eighteen pennylands, in each of which were four mark or farthing lands. A larger unit, the *ursland,* or *eyrisland,* was responsible under the Vikings for supplying, manning, and equipping one ship for the king's service. It shows how numerous and independent were the old Shetland communities that, when the parish system came in, each of the twelve parishes contained several eyrislands. According to G. M. Nelson's *The Story of Tingwall Kirk,* each eyrisland walled off its separate area in the Tingwall parish graveyard.

In every eyrisland, and perhaps even in the smaller units, was a chapel and Thing place. When the Rev. John Brand visited Shetland in 1700 to inquire on behalf of the Church of Scotland into religious conditions there, he counted at least twenty-four chapels, mostly ruined, on the northernmost island of Unst, twenty-one on Yell, and many others on the smaller islands. Some 120 ancient chapel sites are now recorded in Shetland.

Thing sites were probably just as numerous. Often, they gave their name to their district, so in Shetland many parishes have names with a "–ting" ending, such as Nesting, Delting, Aithsting, Lunnasting, and so on. At the hub of them all is the former Shetland Al-thing at Tingwall.

The Shetland Al-Thing

Four miles west of Shetland's capital, Lerwick, is the Loch of Tingwall. From north to south, it is long and narrow, and at its northern end are Tingwall church and village. If you walk through the village toward the church, the loch comes into sight below you, together with something that it is worth going a long way to visit. It is a round, grassy holm, or islet, about sixty feet wide, connected to the shore across large, flat boulders. The causeway is about 140 feet long, and before the eighteenth century, when the level of the loch was artificially lowered to provide more grazing land, it ran across shallow water.

This islet is the Law Ting Holm, formerly and from time immemorial the site of the all-Shetland parliament and law court. Now it is deserted, grazed by sheep and approached with difficulty through fields and over fences to the beginning of the causeway. It is said that there was once a ring of stone seats upon the holm and that these were removed by the local farmer at about the time when the waters of the loch were lowered; but the site has never been excavated, and it may be that some of the old stones are still there under the turf. It would hardly have been worthwhile hauling them away for the sake of a few square feet of extra grazing land.

A vein of white quartz runs through the islet in line with the causeway, outcropping near the center to form what might have been the Lawman's rock. From there, you can see right down the central rift of Mainland to its southernmost cliffs.

Figure 6. At a rare moment when the Loch of Tingwall was in flood, Shetlander Neil Anderson took this photograph of the Law Holm as it was before the eighteenth century, when the waters of the loch were lowered. Over the causeway of stepping-stones, linking the islet to the mainland, plaintiffs and criminals approached the circle of judges on the Law Holm.

The exact nature of the proceedings on the Tingwall Holm are no longer known. In 1611, when Scottish law was imposed on Shetland in place of the old Norse code, the Shetland Law Book mysteriously disappeared, and a unique record of the ancient forms and traditions was lost forever. From what is known of other Shetland Things, it is likely that the chief lawman gave rulings on legal matters from the central rock, while the *foud,* or chief magistrate, presided over the court. The number of judges was strictly limited by the size of the holm. Possibly there were twenty-four of them, consisting of the foud for each of twelve main Thing districts, together with his lawman.

Every *odaller,* or free landholder, of Shetland was expected to attend the Tingwall assembly, which took place over a week at high

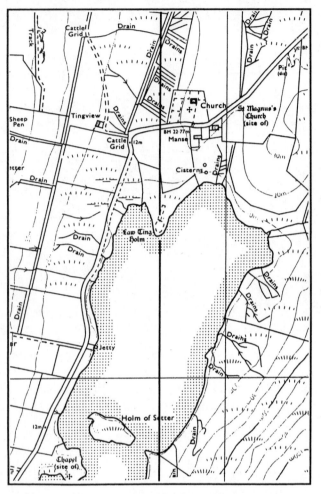

Figure 7. On the six-inch map, the Shetland Law Ting Holm
is shown as it is now, a protrusion into the loch of Tingwall.
It marks the midpoint of Mainland's north–south axis.

summer on the lowlands north of the loch, opposite the entrance to
the Law Holm. They came from all quarters, those from the northern
isles leaving their boats at Cat Firth to the northeast, others riding
along the old, direct path from Scalloway Harbor, three miles away
to the southwest. Their guiding landmark was the peaked mountain
Ward of Laxfrith to the north of Tingwall, which looks likely to have
been the symbolic guardian of the site.

On a raised mound a few hundred yards north of the Law Holm stands the plain church of St. Magnus. It was one of only three Shetland churches that possessed a tower, built of red sandstone from Orkney; but in 1788 this was demolished, for reasons of Puritanism and to provide stone for road making. The present church replaced an ancient chapel, the remains of which can be seen forming a crypt in the graveyard. In front of it, the odallers gathered, and whoever was summoned to the court stepped across the causeway onto the holm. A tradition recorded by Martin Martin in his *Description of the Western Isles of Scotland* is that if a man who had been sentenced to death could escape from the islet and make his way through the crowd to the church, he was allowed to go free. This, of course, would only be possible if the people were sympathetic to his case, so the custom provided a sort of popular court of appeal. The same tradition occurs elsewhere in Shetland, at the old church of Baliasta, near the former Thing site of the northernmost island.

The Tingwall Holm law court was certainly far older than the first known reference to it, in the thirteenth century. Meetings were held there throughout the sixteenth century, the last great event, in 1577, being an assembly of 760 enraged Shetlanders protesting, successfully, against a corrupt and tyrannical foud. In 1600, the ruler of the isles, Patrick Stewart, Earl of Orkney, built Scalloway Castle and removed the Law Thing from its traditional islet to a field beside his new stronghold. Thus, he could and did control its proceedings. A similar fate has been the end of many open-air, democratic assemblies. The Shetland Thing did not long survive its uprooting. Within a few years its law book had gone, and it was extinguished.

Why Did They Meet in the Loch?

In his book, *Orkney and Shetland,* Eric Linklater raises an obvious, practical question about the council on Tingwall Loch's islet. Why, he asks, did the elders of Shetland choose "the windiest and least comfortable of places for their deliberations?" The answer is essentially geographical. It was because someone, in some distant but unknown period, made an accurate survey of Shetland's Mainland in order to discover its exact central point. The appropriate spot was halfway along the main axis of Mainland, the line between its northern and southern extremities, and it so happens that the midpoint of that line is at the Law Ting Holm, the islet in the loch.

The Mainland island of Shetland is shaped like a dagger, with its point at Sumburgh Head in the south and its butt at Mio Ness almost due north. The distance between these two points is forty-four miles. Strictly speaking, the northernmost point of Mainland is in the district of North Maven, to the northwest of Mio Ness, but North Maven is virtually a separate island, being joined to Mainland by a narrow isthmus, no more than sixty yards across, called Mavis Grind. Over this strip of land, the Vikings used to draw their boats, meaning, according to their custom, that North Maven had the status of an island. This is made plain in the *Orkneyinga Saga,* written in about 1200. It tells how King Malcolm of Scotland allowed the Norwegian King Magnus Barelegs to claim all the Scottish islands west of the mainland. The definition of an island was that a ship could pass all around it. King Magnus laid claim to Kintyre, a large, fertile peninsula with a thin neck of land connecting it to the rest of Scotland, and proved his point by sitting at the helm of a boat while his followers dragged it across the isthmus. Thus, Kintyre was represented as an island, and by the same reasoning, the drawing of boats across Mavis Grind insulated North Maven from Mainland.

The discovery that Shetland's Law Ting lies on the main north–south axis of Mainland at exactly the same distance, 22.24 miles, from each end, implies that the spot was chosen by a surveyor. This precise location could scarcely have been hit upon by chance, and the other examples given here, of important Thing sites located similarly within their territories, prove that the Shetland surveyor was following an established practice in finding the precise center

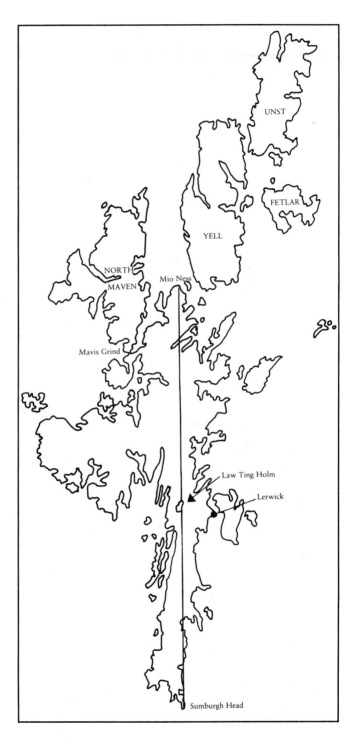

Figure 8. The
north–south axis of
Shetland's Mainland
(excluding the near-
island of North
Maven) has its
midpoint at the exact
spot where, on an
islet in the Loch of
Tingwall, the chief
men of each district
held court and
administered justice.

of Mainland for the site of its Al-thing. The question is, when and by whom was Mainland's central point so carefully calculated? Were they Scandinavian or earlier, Pictish land surveyors? This question is overshadowed by a larger one. Both the Celts and the Norsemen had their traditional systems of ritual land division, similar in detail and based on the same principles. The greater question is, how and from where did they both separately acquire their common code of esoteric science?

The Shetland Thing Circuit

Leading up to the grand midsummer assembly at Tingwall, the court of judges made a circuit of the provincial Thing places. This custom survived into the eighteenth century, and there are records of it over three years from 1602, when the effective ruler and chief justice of Shetland was Earl Patrick Stewart. Beginning at Sumburgh in the far south, he proceeded northward with his retinue by way of Burra, Bressay, Walls, Aithsting, and Delting to the islands of Fetlar and Unst, finishing in the middle of August, when the main Lawthing was held. The next year, he started out on June 9 and completed the circuit on July 15, and in 1604 the process lasted from June 20 to August 20, with the Lawthing six days later. This casual observation of dates was probably for the earl's own convenience, in defiance of settled custom. In earlier periods, the Al-thing would have been held on a regular day, with fixed dates for each of the provincial assemblies and a more extended circuit of Thing places than in Stewart's time.

A long, learned article by Dr. S. Hibbert, "The Ting-sites of Orkney and Shetland" in *Archaeologia Scotica,* from 1831, gives many details of these institutions. The earliest Things, he says, were at or beside the *hof,* the local pagan temple. When Christianity came in, a chapel replaced the hof, and the religious element was transferred from the Thing to the church. Yet many of the pagan forms were still observed. The magic ritual for sanctifying the court began with "fencing" it—defining its area by a temporary, measured perimeter of ropes, stakes, or whatever was customary. Next came the proclamation of the grid. This was a spell or mantra, so solemn that only the officiating priest was ever allowed to utter it, that dedicated the space to Odin—or, later, to the Christian God—and invoked his curse upon whoever broke the peace within it. The judges were summoned by an axe or staff carried round to each of their houses. They were duly sworn in, and the court was opened. In Christian times, the entrance to the Thing was generally in the east, and the lawman faced in that direction while giving judgment. Originally, according to pagan custom, he would probably have faced south.

The Shetland Thing sites inspected by Hibbert were marked by concentric rings of loosely piled stones with a heap or pillar in the middle. Two rings were sufficient for a local Thing, three rings defining the more important sites. These divisions separated the inner court from the surrounding landholders, the plaintiffs, and the public at large.

About the actual locations of the old Shetland Things, Hibbert is sadly vague. His crude map (figure 9) gives approximate positions only, and his identifications of sites are mostly speculative. The fact is that most of the old Thing places in Shetland, Orkney, and elsewhere have long been forgotten. Certain traditions about former Thing sites are known to local scholars, but there has been little research, and most identifications are tentative. The level of information is typified by this entry in the *Inventory of Shetland,* compiled by the Scottish Royal Commission for Ancient Monuments: "A circular, grass-covered and partly artificial mound of sand situated by the side of the Kirkhouse Burn, about 120 yards south of the farmhouse of Setter, is reputed to have been the meeting-place of the Ting of Delting." Even this degree of certainty is rare.

Since every local Thing imitated the national center, which was itself modeled on the assembly of gods around the pole of the world-tree, it is reasonable to suppose that each of them was similarly located on the symbolic pole at the center of its territory. It should therefore be possible to rediscover the Thing site for any given region. The trouble is that to define a Thing district, one has to know its original boundaries. That limits our inquiry to islands, where boundaries are fixed by nature and scarcely change over hundreds of years.

After Mainland, the three largest of the Shetland islands are the northern group—Unst, Fetlar, and Yell. Unst, the nearest island to Norway, is thought to have been the first place of Viking settlement and the site of the earliest Shetland Thing, mentioned in the *Orkneyinga Saga*. Three different spots are claimed as the original Thing place. Near the south of the island, the recumbent Stone of Hamarberg at Gunnister, shaped very like a Cornish pasty and strangely carved with a series of shallow pits, is a traditional site of the first Shetland law court. Further north, high up on Crussafield Hill, a group of cairns was identified by Hibbert as an ancient ritual center. One of them, a stone heap surrounded by three concentric rings of earth, fitted his idea of an important Thing place. The others, he thought, were designed for lesser assemblies. Below the hill is the ancient, ruined church at Baliasta. Like Tingwall Church, it has the legend that a criminal, condemned at the Thing, could find refuge there—if he could escape from the court and evade his pursuers. Somewhere near the church was the third traditional site, a stone ring. It has long been destroyed, and its exact position is no longer known.

The main axis of Unst is the longest line one can draw through it, from its southernmost point to its central northern headland, the Noup. Halfway along the line is a spot (O.S. reference 605089; from the British Ordnance Survey map system) south of Baliasta Church where two or three lowstanding stones, with others fallen, seem to mark an ancient enclosure. It commands a wide view of the surrounding country and looks like a most suitable spot for the central Thing. There is no proof of this, however, and one can assert no further than

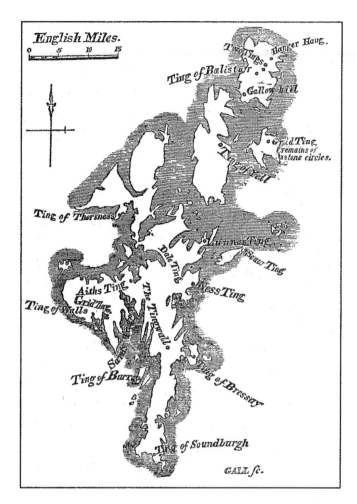

Figure 9. Hibbert's map of 1831 illustrated his research into Shetland Thing places. Though primitive and inaccurate, it indicates the positions of several sites now forgotten, as in the islands of Unst, Yell, and Bressay.

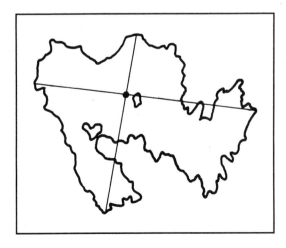

Figure 10. The Shetland island of Fetlar; the axes between its extremities, north, south, east, and west, cross at the center where, in the 1830s, surveyor James Irving located the Fetlar Thing place.

that the Unst Thing was formerly held approximately on the halfway point of the axis, near the church of refuge at Baliasta.

Fetlar is a fertile island but now sadly depopulated. Once it contained hundreds of families, many of whom were evicted in the nineteenth century to make room for sheep, and it is famous for the wealth of its folklore. Legends tell of the magical Finn people and how they built the mysterious great wall, the Finnigord, that runs from north to south across the island and divides it into two almost equal halves. On the west side of the Finnigord is the island's airstrip, and there once stood the "Ting or green knoll" that was pointed out to James Irving, who surveyed Fetlar in 1832, as the main Fetlar Thing. Near it to the northeast are two stone rings that Hibbert noted as typical Thing sites. One of these, named Hyltadance, is on the direct line between the northernmost and southernmost points of the island, and where this line cuts the main axis, the longest line that can be drawn across the territory, is the approximate site of Irving's Thing mound, placed at the symbolic center of the island.

In the case of Yell, Shetland's second largest island, Hibbert's map shows a Thing near its center at Mid Yell. The main north–south axis of Yell has its midpoint there, but the exact spot has nothing interesting to show. Robert Johnson of Mid Yell says that local tradition indicates a low mound at Setter as a former Thing place. It is likely that the main Thing of Yell was about a mile to the east of this, near the old ruined church of Mid Yell. In that case, it would have been approximately on the main axis but not precisely halfway along it.

It must often have happened that the most obvious symbolic center of an island was found to be unsuitable as a place of assembly. In that case, it was necessary to compromise, to dilute the principle of central location with other geomantic considerations. This subject calls for deeper studies by local scholars who know their country and are interested in discovering its ancient center.

The Pole of Orkney

The nine or so principal Orkney islands, with many lesser companions, have a smaller combined area than Shetland, 375 square miles, but they are fifty miles farther south and generally more fertile. In these richer lands, where local democracies fell more readily under the power of landlords, the old Norse traditions have been thoroughly eroded by centuries of Scottish and English dominance, and even less Thing lore has survived than in Shetland. Two place-names in Orkney's Mainland—Tingwall, eight miles northwest of Kirkwall, and Dingieshowe (Thing mound), the same distance to the southeast—indicate former Thing sites. Hibbert and other old writers identify the megalithic Stones of Stenness ring as an important pre-Christian place of assembly. All that is known for certain is that from the late twelfth century, when Kirkwall, the present capital, became the main residence of the Earls of Orkney, the national Thing met there, possibly on the green beside the cathedral. Dedicated to the martyred chieftain, St. Magnus, and containing his relics, Kirkwall Cathedral was the most holy sanctuary in the Northern Isles.

For practical purposes, Kirkwall is the ideal center of Orkney. It is easily accessible from all the islands, has a fine harbor, and is strategically situated on a neck of land between the east and west parts of the largest, most populous island, now called Mainland. Formerly, it was known more euphoniously as Pomona. No wonder Kirkwall was made the capital. It seems needless to explain such an obviously suitable place in terms of mystical geography. Yet from the example of Shetland, repeated in the Faroes and other islands, it is reasonable to suspect that Orkney, too, would have had its symbolic pole passing through its ceremonial center.

Orkney's polar axis is easily identified. From the southern tip of the southernmost inhabitable island, Brough Ness in South Ronaldsay, the meridian line is drawn north. It runs to Bow Head, the northernmost point of the most northern of the main islands,

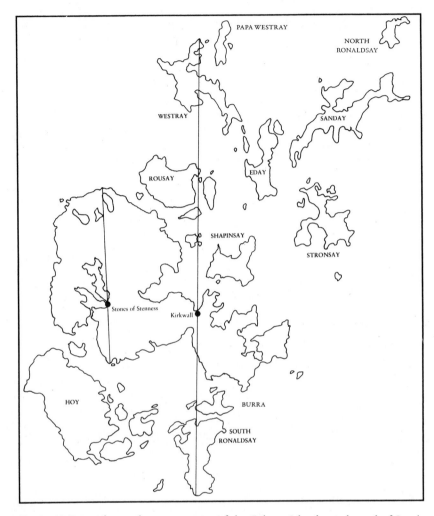

Figure 11. From the southernmost point of the Orkney Islands, at the end of South Ronaldsay, the meridian axis extends to the northern point of Westray. On it, beside the cathedral at Kirkwall, is the probable site of the main Orkney Thing. Another reputed Thing place is at the Stones of Stenness, one of the famous megalithic monuments in that part of Mainland. The Stones are sited on the north–south axis of the district.

Westray. Two small islands, Papa Westray and North Ronaldsay, are at higher latitudes, but this line forms the meridian axis of the whole group. It passes through Kirkwall, slightly to the east of the cathedral. Thereabouts would have been the site of the Al-thing.

When the Orkney and Shetland groups are seen on the same map, it is apparent that their main axes are aligned by nature on the meridian and parallel to each other.

Several of the Orkney islands have an obvious axis that may have determined the placing of their Thing sites. In Eday, for example, the north–south axis has its halfway point beside the Loch of Doomy. The name indicates the proximity of a Law Thing, but the site is now the island airfield.

As for the Stones of Stenness, they lie in the bulk of Mainland, west of Kirkwall. Typically for a Thing place, they are on a headland between two lochs. They are also on the north–south axis of their district, the line between Houton Head in the south and the furthest point north. There, perhaps, was the ancient Thing for West Pomona.

The Thing on Loch Finlaggan

It is a moot point whether the Thing on Shetland's Tingwall Holm was established there by the Norsemen or whether they took it over from the previous, Pictish administration. Some light may be shed on the matter by comparing it with another, very similar islet court in the Hebridean island of Islay.

Islay and the other Western Islands were conquered and settled in the ninth century by Norwegian chiefs who found it necessary to leave their own country to escape the centralizing tyranny of King Harald Fairhair. In 866, King Harald made an expedition to assert his authority over the rebellious colonists. Before returning home, he placed the Hebrides (known to the Norsemen as the Sudreyjar, or Sudreysor Southern Islands) under a viceroy who also governed the Isle of Man.

The Sudreys and Man soon became, for all practical purposes, an independent kingdom. Toward the end of the eleventh century, its king, Godred Crovan, ruled widely in Scotland and Ireland, including

Dublin, but in 1263 the Hebridean Norsemen were defeated by the Scots, and the Western Islands came under the Scottish crown.

Under the Norsemen, the Hebrides were administered as four separate provinces, with centers on Lewis, Skye, Mull, and Islay. No doubt they established Things in every small island and district, but none of these sites seem to be known for certain, nor is it known where the Council of Island Chiefs had their original Al-thing meetings. It is likely to have been on an island between the northern and southern limits of their kingdom, that is, between the north of Lewis and the south of the Isle of Man. It may well have been on Colonsay, which was the first center of the Norse government.

Even after their defeat by the Scots, the Norse nobility continued as local rulers of the isles, intermarrying with Scottish families and adopting Gaelic names and customs. One of them, Macdonald of Islay, rose to prominence and in the late fourteenth century was proclaimed Lord of the Isles. He and his descendants reigned from their Islay stronghold until 1493, when the lordship was abolished. Rebel Macdonalds made several attempts to revive it, but in 1748, after the failure of Bonnie Prince Charlie, the Scottish chiefs were stripped of their powers, and local independence was extinguished.

From the time of Macdonald's lordship, the traditional place of judgment on Islay became the annual meeting place for the Council of Island Chiefs. It was a tiny islet in Loch Finlaggan, Eilean na Comhairle, or Council Island. Measuring no more than thirty yards across, it was connected by a stone causeway to a larger island, Eilean Mor, on which stood the castle and official residence of the Macdonalds, the family burial ground, and the chapel of St. Finlaggan. Another causeway, from the north of this island, led to the shore, where the Macdonald guards had their houses.

The whole place is now desolate and in ruins. Only traces remain of the old causeways, and if you want to go to the Council Island, you have to swim or find a boat. Of the once-great castle, nothing survives but some foundations, now overgrown. Council Island is a wilderness

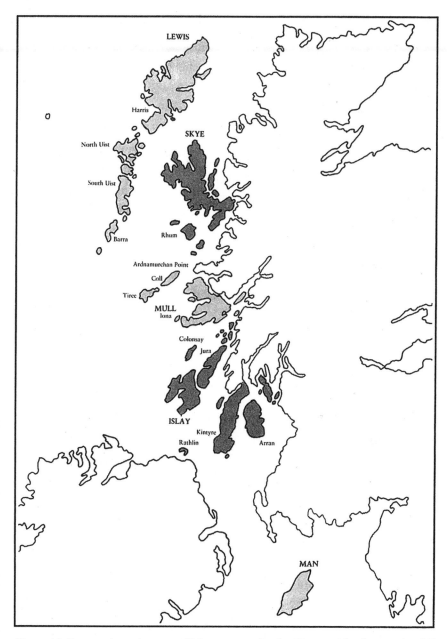

Figure 12. From at least the time of Norwegian rule, the Western Islands were divided into four groups and formed a united kingdom with the four quarters of the Isle of Man. The four main islands were Lewis, Skye, Mull, and Islay, and the officially counted number of islands in the kingdom was thirty-two.

of tall grass and flowers. Two small rectangular areas, shown on the map, were probably connected with the "counsell-house" mentioned in Donald Monro's seventeenth-century account. From this, it appears that the island chiefs lapsed from the ancient custom of meeting in the open air.

Membership on the council was based on the four-part division of the islands. According to Monro, it consisted of the four ruling lords, four thanes or lesser chiefs, and four others of royal blood—twelve in all—with two additional members, the bishop and the abbot of Icolmkill.

Hugh Macdonald of Skye, writing in about 1630, said that there were sixteen councillors: four thanes, four armins (subthanes), four bastards (squires or small estate owners), and four freeholders or farmers with their own land. The original idea seems to have been that each quarter sent its chief with two or three retainers representing different classes of landowners. Thus, even at this late date, the Hebridean Al-thing retained its democratic character, the four great chiefs being balanced by equal numbers of lesser notables and small independent farmers.

The council managed the internal affairs of the isles, issued charters, and provided a land registry. It also constituted a supreme court. Every island had its judge, paid by the Macdonalds, from whose court appeals could be made to the council on Loch Finlaggan. A traditional duty of the council was to ensure the accuracy of weights and measures. There is mention of a *lapadis M'Coull,* the standard weight for all the islands.

The most solemn meeting on Loch Kinlaggan was for the purpose of electing (or occasionally dismissing) a lord of the isles. After his election, he was installed in the full panoply of kingship. Hugh Macdonald gave a most interesting account of this ceremony.

I thought fit to annex the ceremony of proclaiming the Lord of the Isles. At this the Bishop of Argyle, the Bishop of the Isles, and seven priests, were sometimes present; but a bishop was always present, with the chieftains of all the principal families, and a *Ruler of the Isles*. There was a square stone, seven or eight feet long, and the tract of a man's foot cut thereon, upon which he stood, denoting that he should walk in the footsteps and uprightness of his predecessors, and that he was installed by right in his possessions. He was clothed in a white habit, to shew his innocence and integrity of heart, that he would be a light to his people, and maintain the true religion. The white apparel did afterwards belong to the poet by right. Then he was to receive a white rod in his hand, intimating that he had power to rule, not with tyranny and partiality, but with discretion and sincerity. Then he received his forefathers' sword, or some other sword, signifying that his duty was to protect and defend them from the incursions of their enemies in peace or war, as the obligations and customs of his predecessors were. The ceremony being over, mass was said after the blessing of the bishop and seven priests, the people pouring their prayer for the success and prosperity of their new created Lord. When they were dismissed, the Lord of the Isles feasted them for a week thereafter; gave liberally to the monks, poets, bards and musicians. You may judge that they spent liberally without any exceptions of persons.

Martin Martin, in his *Description of the Western Isles,* written in about 1695, adds that during the ceremony of anointing the new lord, "the orator rehearsed a catalogue of his ancestors etc."

The whole ceremony could hardly have changed since pagan times. The bishop had replaced the chief Druid, but the ruler still wore the white druidic robe and was invested with the ancient symbolic rod and sword. His foot was placed in the footprint of the first divine ruler, seven holy men officiated, and the event included a seven-day festival of bards. These were features of Celtic installation ritual in its most archaic form.

Figure 13. Upon the stone of installation, on an islet in Loch Finlaggan, the Lord of the Isles ruled through a council of chiefs. The Macdonald Lord in his ceremonial costume is shown in this nineteenth-century engraving.

Islay's Tingwall

The table of stone at which the council sat and the flagstone with the ancestral footprint were carried off by the Earl of Argyll in about 1615. The castle, chapel, houses, and all buildings at Loch Finlaggan fell into ruins, and the site is now described as bleak and depressing. I. F. Grant, who went there in 1934, found it "disappointing" and called Finlaggan an "uninteresting loch." R. W. Munro, in his edition of *Monro's Western Isles of Scotland,* comments that "anyone familiar with the rugged grandeur of Thingvellir in Iceland, or with the Tynwald Hill in the Isle of Man, will look in vain at Finlaggan or Tingwall for any parallel with these other historic centres of the old Viking world." In other words, the Al-thing site at Finlaggan is not at all picturesque. Yet Grant notes that the peaks of the dominant local mountains, the Paps of Jura, are visible from there to the east. The qualities of the place are evidently more symbolic than aesthetic.

Once more arises the question of why such a strikingly inconvenient spot should have been identified as the center of Islay and become the hallowed place of assembly for the all-islands council. As elsewhere, the reason is, at least in part, geographical. Council Island lies adequately upon the pole and main axis of Islay, the twenty-four-mile-long line between its northernmost and southernmost points. This indicates that the islet was the ritual cent of Islay alone and not originally of all the islands.

Unlike Tingwall in Shetland, which is exactly halfway along the Mainland axis, Finlaggan is by no means central. Nor is its position on the axis quite precise. The point on the northern coast of Islay where the line from the southern point through Council Isle terminates is about 350 yards west of the most northern rock. One could say, of course, that a good storm might at any time have removed the few square yards of rock that once made the terminus of the axis coincide with the northernmost point, but taking the facts as they are, it seems that whoever first picked out Council Island was prepared to

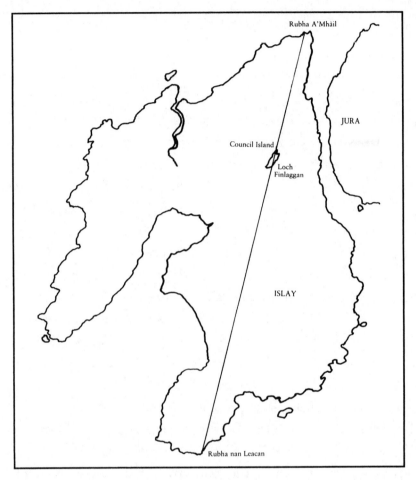

Figure 14. From the southernmost point of Islay, the twenty-five-mile-long axis through Council Island in Loch Finlaggan ends slightly to the west of the northern extremity.

compromise between ideal and actual geography, and be content with a site very nearly on Islay's polar axis.

Far from being what now seems to be a disadvantage, the site on a barely accessible islet in a lonely loch must have been highly attractive to the people who chose it—so attractive that they were prepared to overlook its inadequacies as a meeting place. Munro and others have commented on the similarity between Finlaggan's Council Island and Law Holm in the loch at Tingwall in Shetland. It is indeed striking.

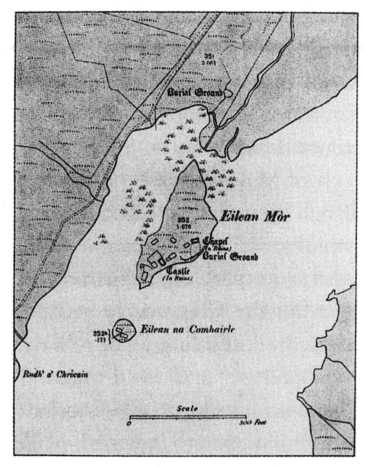

Figure 15. Only about 100 feet wide, Council Island in Islay's Loch Finlaggan was the center of law and justice for the Western Isles. Between this island and the shore, once linked to both by stone causeways, is the larger island where the Macdonald Lord of Islay and the Western Isles had his castle.

The islets are both virtually the same size and shape and occupy similar positions in similar lochs. Even the design of the stone causeways, laid in both cases along the north–south axis toward the islets, follows the same principle. There seems to be no mythological or other good reason why a court or council should he held on an island in a loch. One of the two sites, Tingwall or Finlaggan, must surely have been chosen in imitation of the other.

That, of course, means that Finlaggan was an imitation of Tingwall. The Shetland Law Holm was made the ritual center, not because it was an island but because it happened to be the ideal spot, halfway along the polar axis of Mainland. Islay's Council Island is also on the main axis, but not quite perfectly so, and nowhere near the most central or convenient place for the island assembly. Tingwall was clearly the prototype, and the surveyors or geomancers who decided to locate the Islay center in Loch Finlaggan sacrificed all other principles in finding a copy of the Tingwall islet.

Islay's Council Island is doubtless a very old site. The archaic Celtic nature of its forms and traditions suggest that it was a place of ritual long before the Norsemen came. In that case, if the Tingwall center is even older, it must originally have been a Celtic or Pictish rather than a Viking foundation.

3

WHY THE ALTING MET AT TÓRSHAVN

Things of Faroe

The sixteen inhabited isles of Faroe lie between Scotland and Iceland, two hundred miles northwest of their nearest neighbor, Shetland. The two island groups are remarkably similar, both tailing off at southern points, called Sumba and Sumburgh, and both having almost the same areas of land, Faroe at 540 square miles, Shetland, 551.

Culturally, however, the positions are rather different. Faroe came under Viking rule in about 870, a hundred years or so later than Shetland, and by the early part of the tenth century, its governing assembly, the Alting, was firmly established at the present capital, Tórshavn. Over the centuries, under political pressure from first Norway and then Denmark, the Alting was stripped of its legislative powers. Renamed in about 1400 the Law Ting (Løgting), it survived as a provincial court with some minor administrative duties until, in 1816, it was abolished altogether. In 1852, the Løgting was revived, and now it is once again the ruling body of Faroe, responsible for all but foreign affairs under the protection of Denmark. For the sake of its valuable fishing rights, Faroe has chosen to remain outside the European Community. Recently, however, the amount of fish left in

Faroese waters has so diminished that the economy of the islands has become dependent on Danish subsidies.

Shetland, in contrast, has known little about self-government since the Law Ting was ejected from its islet. Its ancient institutions have all gone, and unlike Faroese, which is officially recognized and spoken, the old Shetland language, Norn, has long died out. This cultural difference is reflected in the different levels of population. Faroe has almost 50,000 inhabitants, twice as many as Shetland.

The Icelandic Al-thing was founded in 930, but the Faroese version is a few years older, giving it seniority over all other European parliaments. The Manx, however, point out that their parliament, the Tynwald, has existed without a break since at least 979 and is therefore the oldest *continuous* national assembly. It is a moot question—examined later in chapter 4—how long the Manx Tynwald has met at its present site, but there is no doubt that the Ting of all Faroe has always been held at Tórshavn, originally on a flat spit of rock that projects into the harbor and divides it into two halves.

The Alting was first and foremost a religious assembly, held under the protection of Thor. By his authority, it pronounced the laws and upheld them as the supreme court of justice. While it was in session—in spring, at midsummer, and occasionally at other times as required—bonfires blazed atop the four hills on each side of it. Every freeman on the islands was obliged to attend its sessions, and the thirty-six "best men" of the Faroes, six from each of the six local Thing districts, made up the panel of judges. An elected lawman served as their speaker and president.

Comparing this system with the constitution of old Iceland, described later in this chapter, shows that both were derived from the same prototype and were in fact identical, except that the Faroese administration was on a smaller scale.

The provincial Things were called Vartings, implying that they met in spring. Beginning on the first day of March on the western island, Vágar, the succession of Vartings moved clockwise round the islands, to Stremoy, Esturoy, Bordoy, Sandoy, and Suduroy, with the Alting following at midsummer. The lawman and his servants also went round, for he had to attend all these meetings.

A similar round of meetings still takes place within each of the six districts of Faroe. Earlier in the year, before each Varting, the district lawman and his two officers make a circuit of the small communities, holding court in each and deciding on local disputes. The members of these minor courts are the village freeholders.

There is something very appealing to one's sense of order and symmetry in the idea of a simple pattern running through and linking every level of administration. The ideals of equal shares for all and equal participation in public affairs—local, regional, and national—gave to the early republic of the Faroes many of the qualities that Plato wished upon the citizens of his proposed city-state. Nor is this surprising, since both constitutions, Platonic and Faroese, were drawn from the same esoteric tradition of a perfectly ordered universe and its eternal pole. The simple folk of old Faroe had no kings, courthouses, government buildings, or national monuments. Their equal freeholders decided everything in common, in accordance with their foundation laws, and the whole law code was deposited in the memory of their elected lawman. At the center of their country, constitution, and collective world-picture, the lynchpin of their orderly existence, was the Rock of Tinganes, where the Alting sat.

The Rock of Tinganes

It has always been a complete mystery why the Norse farmers who colonized the Faroe islands chose as their national center the exposed, windy finger of rock at Tórshavn. For at least two centuries before their arrival, the islands had been inhabited by Irish monks who lived by farming and fishing, so it is possible that the newcomers inherited some of their traditions, including the sacred Rock of Tinganes.

Figure 16. Tinganes at Tórshavn, the rock that divides the harbor into two parts, as it is today.

Whoever chose it seems at first sight to have made a bad decision. Its position is conveniently central, but as the hub of a nation that depends on trade and shipping, it is poorly adapted. There are many better harbors in Faroe. In fact, Tórshavn has only recently, by extensive jetties and engineering works, been made to function as a port. Commenting on this in their book, *The Faroe Islands,* Liv Kjørsvik Schei and Gunnie Moberg say that Tórshavn is "not

Figure 17 (opposite). The meridian axis of the Faroe islands, from the southern end of Suduroy to the northern tip of Kalsoy, passes through Tinganes, the spit of rock that projects into the harbor at Tórshavn. On that rock was the site of the Faroese Alting.

Also shown are the main axes of Sandoy and Suduroy islands. In both cases, the island Ting place or its temple was placed at the midway point.

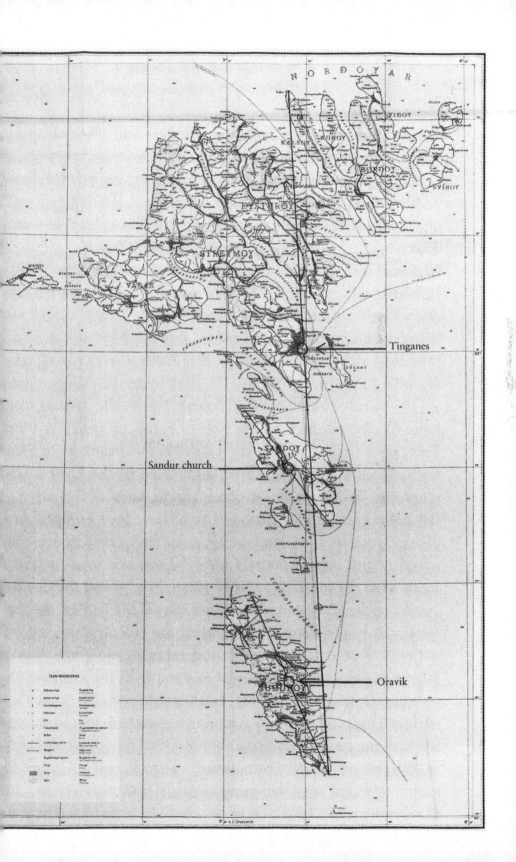

Tinganes

Sandur church

Oravik

naturally protected but is wide open to storms from the south-east" and that there have always been complaints about its inadequate harbor. Without the status given to it by the Rock of Tinganes, Tórshavn would never have flourished. Four hundred years ago, it had no more than a hundred inhabitants, and it did not really become a town before the twentieth century.

For all its practical defects, the image of Tórshavn as the universal center is firmly fixed within the Faroese world-picture. This is made clear by the authors of *The Faroe Islands,* quoting the famous Tórshavn writer and reviver of Faroese culture, William Heinesen. "Tórshavn does not excel through visual beauty, a unique location or unusual achievements. It is only a small town between sea, mountain and moor. But this spot is not just the capital of a tiny island country; it is really also the navel of the world!"

The navel of Faroe must, of course, receive the Faroese world-pole. As seen on the map, the pole of Faroe, or rather its world-tree, grows upward from the southernmost headland at Sumba on Suduroy. The straight line from there to the northernmost point, on Vidoy, fails on three counts to provide either the symbolic pole or the national omphalos. It does not form a dividing axis for the island group; apart from crossing a northern island, it runs almost entirely over the sea; and it is inclined far away from the meridian. On all these three points, the line from Sumba to the secondmost northern spot in the Faroes, the top of Kalsoy, is better adapted to represent the pole. It also locates the national center. This should preferably be on Streymoy, the largest and most central island. For some miles, the Sumba–Kalsoy pole passes through Streymoy, and aligned on that stretch is the Rock of Tinganes. The pole runs down the length of Tinganes and through the center of Tórshavn.

Why this exposed promontory was preferred to somewhere more sheltered on the same axis is still mysterious. It is characteristic of Thing sites in general to be surrounded by water, on peninsulas, headlands, or islets. For some good geomantic reason, or combination of reasons including its situation on the pole, priestly surveyors recognized Tinganes as the symbolic center of Faroe, and upon it they based their constitution, their state ritual and institutions, and the entire order of their lives.

The Løgting no longer sits in the fresh air on Tinganes, but in a fine parliament building nearby, built for it in 1856. Fishing is in decline, the islands' economy has suffered, and ambitious people in Tórshavn are naturally drawn to the greater center in Copenhagen. Clearly, the old rock has lost power and is not the all-engrossing center it once was. Yet it is the basic national symbol, impossible to replace. Every Faroese knows what to answer if asked to name the center of the islands: Tinganes at Tórshavn.

The Island Things

In the early days there were many local Things throughout the Faroe islands. Every *bygd* (small village) had one. Despite their Viking ancestry, many of the old islanders felt no urge to travel, even as far as Tórshavn, but were content with the world-center located in their own communities. The authors of *The Faroe Islands* tell of a woman living recently on the far northeast island of Fugloy, which has just two *bygdir,* who at the age of over seventy had not only never left the island but had never even seen the other village a few miles away.

Very few of the smaller Thing sites are now known, but in his early history of the Faroes, *From the Vikings to the Reformation: A Chronicle of the Faroe Islands up to 1538,* G. V. C. Young gives information on the six local Vartings that, like their counterparts in Iceland, probably met before and after the Alting, in spring and late summer. They met one after the other on the six largest islands, and their sites were as follows:

The Thing on Vágar met at Midvágar; on Streymoy at Kollafjørdur on an islet in the fjord; on Esturoy at Selatrad, but in earlier times at Stevnavalur; on Bordoy at Vágur (now Klaksvik); on Sandoy at Sandur; and on Suduroy at Oravik.

To pinpoint all these sites, it would be necessary to visit all the various islands. Ideally, one would expect to find them half-way along the north–south axis of each island or island group, but the map shows that in some cases the central spot is high on a mountain, unsuitably placed for assemblies. In two cases, however, where the lie of the land was favorable, the rule seems to have been obeyed.

On Suduroy, the southernmost island, the halfway point on the main axis is about a mile outside Oravik, just where the authors of *The Faroe Islands* locate it. "On the mountain slope above the *bygd* the local Ting for Suduroy used to assemble. The Tingstead was known as Uppi Imillum Stovur and the site was probably chosen because it formed a natural amphitheatre ideally suited to the purpose, and because it was centrally located."

The most interesting example is on Sandoy, the most fertile of the islands, with a population of about 1,800. Its Thing was at Sandur, which is still the administrative center. The church there was built in 1839, but the site is one of the oldest in the islands. Excavations in 1969 revealed that it was preceded on the same site by no less than five earlier churches, beginning with a small wooden shrine of the early eleventh century, when Christianity was introduced. This was the center of the original settlement, and since it is likely that the custom of building each new church on the site of the old goes back to the beginning, the original pagan temple probably stood where the church does now.

Like most of the Faroe Islands, Sandoy extends roughly north-west and southeast. The distance between its northernmost and southernmost tips is about twenty-one miles, and the midway point on that line falls on or just beside the Sandur church. This by itself could simply be chance, but taking it together with the other examples of centrally placed Thing sites, it is strong evidence that the pagan temple that stood near every early Thing place was where the Sandur church stands now. At an adjacent farm, i Trödum, is a stone that traditionally marks the site of the open-air Thing court.

Iceland's Ideal Commonwealth

Like the first American colonists, fleeing persecution at home by sailing westward in the *Mayflower* toward new lands, the first Norwegian settlers of Iceland escaped the tyranny of King Harald Fairhair by moving to a new country in the far West. Their leaders were local chieftains, accustomed to ruling without interference in their own lands, who resented the new king's policy of usurping their powers to create a centralized kingdom. Iceland previously had been inhabited by some communities of Celtic monks. The Norsemen began moving there in 874, and within sixty years, their population had grown to number 50,000.

From the very beginning, mysterious rituals were enacted by those who settled there. On sighting land, the chieftains cast out of their ships the pillars of the high seat in their ancestral temple, which they had carried with them from Norway. They then landed and built temporary shelters before going in search of the pillars. Sometimes this took many years. At the place where they found them, washed up on the shore, they built a new temple with farms and houses beside it. Then began the ritual process of hallowing the country. This included the lighting of bonfires around the borders of the lands they occupied.

The modern Icelandic scholar, Einar Pálsson, has published in his own language a many volume work, *The Roots of Icelandic Culture,* with evidence that the earliest settlers were guided by a previously determined foundation plan. Their code of geomancy had reference to astronomy, land measurement, geography, timekeeping, and astrology, and was governed by a system of symbolic number. According to

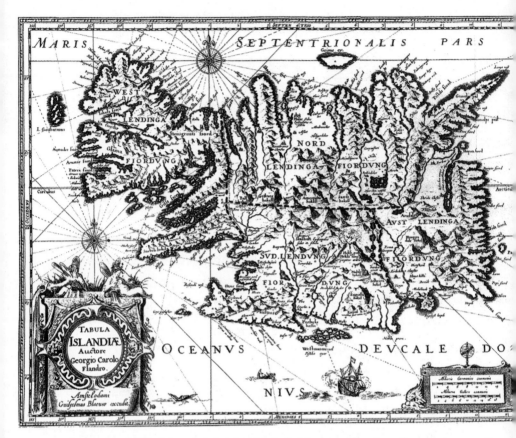

Figure 18. Iceland was divided by the early Norse settlers into four quarters and twelve Thing districts, each with ritualized subdivisions. The central region being inaccessible, the site of the national Al-thing was established in the southwest near Reykjavik.

Pálsson, the number 216,000 (a number examined in the last chapter of this book) was especially prominent.

Pálsson's discovery of an original foundation pattern has caused much controversy among the learned of Iceland, but there are many passages in the Sagas that give evidence of it and that cannot otherwise be interpreted. The Sagas in themselves imply that the whole country was systematically hallowed from the beginning. Their traditional accounts of ancient gods and the deeds of heroes were woven around actual settlements, landmarks, and the names of local families.

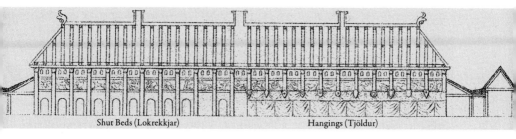

Shut Beds (Lokrekkjar)   Hangings (Tjöldur)

Figure 19. The local chieftain-priests of pagan Iceland lived and feasted in finely carved wooden halls. Fire troughs were ranged down the center, and the general design was as shown in the section below.

Storytellers repeated them as heritage from time immemorial, and their themes were indeed ancient. Their details, however, were localized. A web of stories and legends was laid on the Icelandic landscape, binding together its rocks, rivers, and other natural features with the families who lived there, and thus placing the whole country under the spell of mythology.

With the first farms and temples, Thing places were located in every settlement and then in every district, and a single, unified code of law was upheld in every court. The law code was formalized soon after the completion of settlement, early in the tenth century, by the learned Ulfljótur, who traveled to Norway in order to perfect his knowledge of the Norse traditions. Following the ancient pattern, he confirmed the division of Iceland into four quarters—north, south, east, and west. Each quarter received its own Saga, which was also a chapter in the national Saga, and to each was appointed its own provincial Thing. A court of thirty-six judges met upon its Thingbrekka (hill of laws).

Each quarter was divided into three districts, with Thing places where assemblies were held twice a year, in spring and autumn, and each of these was subdivided into three, making thirty-six Thing courts in all. Justice was administered by a bench of local freemen (*godar*), always numbering twelve or a multiple thereof. The smallest court was that of the individual *godi,* the head of a household with its dependants and servants, who was also the local priest and led the ceremonies in his family temple.

Up to 930, there was no fixed place for a national assembly, an Al-thing. Ulfljótur's law required such an institution, so he commissioned his foster brother, Grimur Geitskör, to find the appropriate site. In the course of a year, Grimur walked over the whole country to its furthest promontories, surveying and measuring it. Through his agility on the high crags, he acquired the second part of his name, which means "goat-shod." Every household in the island paid him one penny for his labours.

Grimur was naturally looking for the central point of Iceland, but it was impossible in that island to find an assembly place anywhere near the geographical center. The center of Iceland is Europe's only true desert, a high, icy region where no settlement has ever been possible, and where drivers who take the road that crosses it today are obliged to travel in convoys. This terrible place has taken firm hold on the Icelanders' imagination. Legends tell of the trolls and ice giants that infest it, and a long-lasting belief is that somewhere behind its glacial crags lies a warm, verdant oasis, a lost Shangri-la. It is known only to outlaws, who were said to live there under a legendary leader, Fjalla-Eyvindar, Iceland's Robin Hood. He could survive in places where anyone else would perish, and caves and shelters in the central district are pointed out as places where he spent winters with his wife, Hella.

By a combination of practical and geomantic considerations, Grimur discovered the symbolic center, the best possible site for the national Al-thing. Thingvellir (Fields of the Thing) is in the southwest of the island about thirty miles from Reykjavik. It is a rocky, fissured, lava-strewn plain, bordered to the east by the major geological rift in the island, through which the river Oxará (Axewater) flows to its outlet in Lake Thingvellir. Pálsson discerns a pattern of symbolic geography that links this site to the main landscape features and old places of settlement in the southwest region, and it is also uniquely

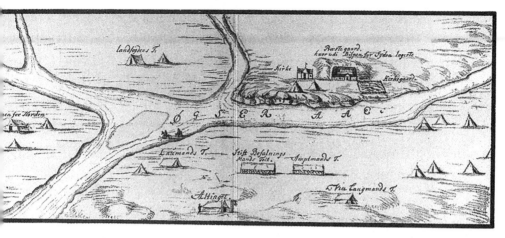

Figure 20. At Thingvellir, beside the river that flows through the great Icelandic rift, the midsummer Al-thing was attended by freemen and their families from all parts of the island. Tents were set up, and the leading families lodged in their own booths. Some features of the assembly are shown in this drawing, made at the beginning of the eighteenth century.

suited to its purpose, awesomely impressive and capable of providing wood, water, and camping places for the thousands who attended the annual Al-thing.

Every freeman of Iceland, with his family and as many retainers as could be spared from farm duties, did his best to go to the Al-thing, which was held over two weeks from the end of June. Some traveled for hundreds of miles, riding their ponies along mountain tracks, guided by stone cairns that their forefathers had set up on hilltops. At Thingvellir, they set up temporary shelters on their accustomed sites, while the most important families lodged in stone booths along the Oxará River. As well as the serious business of judging, legislation, and the execution of criminals, there were fun and games for all. Deals were struck, children were given in marriage, and a festive atmosphere prevailed. When all was done, they rode home again to prepare for the long winter ahead.

Again like the American colonists, the Icelanders rejected the idea of a king, and the head of their nation was the speaker of the law, a

senior scholar with defined, limited functions and no executive powers. His most prominent duty was to recite by heart the entire law
code of Iceland while standing on a rocky pinnacle, the Lögberg (Law
Rock), during the course of the Al-thing assembly. Together with the
body of deputies, drawn equally from the four quarters and thirty-six
Thing districts, he represented the element of sovereignty in the state
constitution.

The supreme Al-thing court seems originally to have consisted
of thirty-six members, but an irregularity arose when the northern
quarter found that, because it was so difficult to travel in the terrain,
they needed four main Thing sites. This increased the North's representation at the Al-thing from nine to twelve members, so the three
other quarters were allowed to nominate three extra members each,
bringing the total number of the court to forty-eight (4 regions × 12
members). Each deputy was then allowed to choose two others, who
ranked equal with him, so the full complement of the Al-thing court
was 144 freemen of Iceland.

This wonderful, mathematical constitution was based on a duodecimal number code that provided the formula for Iceland's foundation plan, its pattern of legal and civil administration, the division
of its lands, and much else besides. No doubt it was also behind the
composition of its music and the Sagas. The basic form of this number code is given here in the last chapter, together with ideas about its
origin and meaning. It produced a society in which, from the tenth
to the thirteenth century, Icelandic culture flourished to become the
wonder of Europe. The farms prospered, deep-water fishing boats
were constructed, the chiefs held feasts in large, finely carved wooden
halls, and the independent, wild-spirited Viking warriors were sub-
ordinated to a law, so rationally and fairly conceived, so simple and
open in its administration, that it was respected by all, even by those
who broke it.

It was indeed a rigorous, inexorable law, comparable to that of
Sparta, carefully defining every individual's rights, duties, and posi-

Figure 21. A "doom ring" at Arnesthing in northern Iceland, where local law was upheld and criminals outlawed or executed.

tion, extending the same degree of discipline to every corner of the country. It was sanctified by Thor, the patron deity of Iceland, and the absolute principle of justice on which it was founded was reflected in its most intricate details. The old Icelandic constitution has been hailed as the very first model democracy, but it was far from being the first of its kind, nor did it allow the universal suffrage that we associate with democracy today. Rather, it was a form of oligarchy, so organized as to give equal representation in its courts to the freemen of every region. Again, as Pálsson points out, it was also a form of monarchy, the crown being represented collectively by the ring of the Al-thing judges and the Speaker of the Law.

The great days of Icelandic culture came to an end in 1264, when the king of Norway took over its government. The Al-thing continued to meet at Thingvellir up to 1798, but the court had lost its old powers, and the event survived mainly as the national festival. Its site and surroundings are now a national park. Iceland became fully independent of Denmark in 1944, and the Al-thing parliament now meets in a hall in Reykjavik.

4

THE CENTER OF THE
ISLE OF MAN

The Manx Tynwald

The Isle of Man is the omphalos of the British Isles. From Langness, its southern peninsula, a circle of less than fifty miles radius touches England, Wales, Ireland, and Scotland, and all these countries are contained within a greater circle that also centers on the Isle of Man. Moreover, the Isle of Man is centrally placed upon the main axis of Britain, the famous line between John o' Groats and Land's End.

In keeping with its significant position, this island has always been known as a place of enchantment. Its legends suggest that once it was a center of the Druidic mysteries. According to Joseph Train's *A Historical Account and Statistical Survey of the Isle of Man,* the chief Druid had his college and residence at Kirk Michael, one of the island parishes. To this place, the kings of Scotland and other Celtic rulers sent their children for education in astronomy, astrology, natural philosophy, and related subjects of traditional learning. One of the few memorials of this period is a Manx ogham inscription, "Of Davaidu the druid's son."

The enchantments of Man are attributed to its patron, Manannan, the Celtic sea god. In his honor, the island has been known successively as Mona, Mana, Mannin, Ellan Vannin, and Mann. His badge,

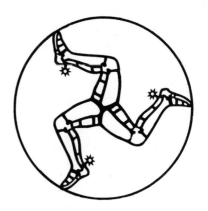

Figure 22. The three-legged symbol of Manannan, the Celtic sea god, patron of the Isle of Man.

and that of Man, is the widely known sun symbol of three running legs within a wheel. The tides, winds, and weather are under his control, and he has been known to raise storms against invaders or to conceal the land from their eyes beneath a cloak of mist. From the days of its Celtic high king, Man has always been a kingdom, the present monarch being Queen Elizabeth II of England. The English dynasty, so the Manx have observed, is not always welcomed by their national deity. Every time during the last hundred years that the island has received a royal visit, the event has been ruined by a sudden storm or blanketing fog.

History provides no records of the early Celtic kings of Man. From the legends of Manannan, whom they personified as sacred rulers, one can infer that they were known as great navigators, traders, magicians, and weather prophets. Their mystical prestige was such that, when Norwegian settlers in the ninth century overwhelmed the native Manx, their leaders were proud to assume the title, Lord of Man. Through them and, after 1266, a succession of Scottish and English rulers, the lordship of Man has lasted up to the present. The island is self-governing, not part of Great Britain or the United Kingdom and not a member of the European Community. It issues its own stamps and coins, and in terms of its population (60,000), it is the smallest island in the world to have a passenger railway system.

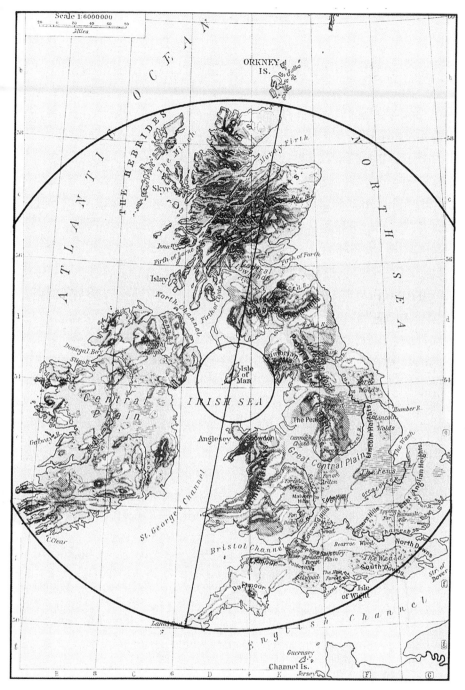

Figure 23. The main axis of the British Isles, from Duncansby Head in Scotland to the Land's End of Cornwall, has its central point on the Isle of Man. A large circle, centered on Man, contains Britain and Ireland, while a smaller circle, 50 miles in radius, touches four countries.

The most remarkable thing about the Isle of Man is its archaic system of administration. It is based on a circular, tiered, artificial mound of earth known as Tynwald. The name, like Iceland's Thingvellir and Shetland's Tingwall, derives from the Norse Ting-Völlir, meaning the Thing field. Manx parliamentary business today is mostly done in a council chamber in the capital, Douglas, but no new laws can be enacted unless they have been openly proclaimed in both Manx and English from the Tynwald mound. Each year, originally at midsummer, now on July 5, the Manx hierarchy arrays itself upon the mound and repeats the time-honored ceremonies. Today, they are mostly formalities, but in earlier days, Tynwald was the ultimate source of authority and elected or confirmed the succession of every Manx ruler.

On the top of the mound, the place once occupied by the Manx king, sits his modern representative, the lieutenant governor. He faces east and by ancient custom should hold his drawn sword, point upright, in front of him. With him, in place of the former chief Druid or high priest of Thor, is the bishop, and in front are the two lawmen or *deemsters* with the legislative council. On the next tier down sit the twenty-four members of the House of Keys, the Manx parliament. Below them are the vicars and captains of each parish, and around the base of the mound are gathered the people of the Isle of Man.

This was originally the Al-thing, the supreme court and legislature, sitting in the open air and the focus for two weeks of an all-island festival. Up to the seventeenth century, lesser courts were held earlier in the year in each of the six *sheading* districts. The governor with his deemsters and other officials would visit them each in turn, beginning at Glenfarba in the central northwest and proceeding clockwise through Michael, Ayre, Garff, and Middle to Rushen in the south.

This arrangement so accurately reproduces the pattern of administration in Iceland, the Faroes, and other Norse colonies that it is

Figures 24 and 25. Two watercolors of about 1795 by John "Warwick" Smith show a distant prospect of St. John's on Tynwald Day, with crowds streaming along the paths toward it, and a closer view of proceedings around the Tynwald mound. The old chapel, now replaced by the steepled church of St. John, is seen on the right.

generally supposed to have been instituted by the Vikings. Their colonial constitutions were based on the Law of Gulating, the traditional code that from very early times was upheld on the Thing mound on the island of Gula in northwest Norway. Unwritten before the twelfth century, it was transmitted orally through a succession of lawmen who each learned it by heart.

With one obvious exception, the Norse and Celtic traditions of government were essentially the same. Access to public affairs was limited to free landholders, but the members of every court and council, from the village to the national level, were elected by the free vote of their peers. The result was a limited, aristocratic form of democracy. In its archaic form, it was also a monarchy with a sovereign king. That was the case in ancient Ireland and Celtic lands generally. In Norway, however, kingship was at some stage abolished, and sovereignty was vested in the lawman, a detached, scholarly figure with no executive powers, whose function was to preside over the national council and provide the ultimate ruling on matters of law.

In Iceland and Faroe, the Viking colonists killed or drove out the few monkish settlers who were there previously, and thus they could start anew, establishing an ideal commonwealth under the Law of Gulating. In the Isle of Man, they had to compromise with existing customs, including the Manx tradition of kingship. This was certainly a native Celtic institution, and the fact of its survival throughout the period of Norse rule opens the question of how many other elements in the traditional Manx constitution, including its land divisions and assembly places, were adopted by the Norsemen from the previous Celtic system.

Dividing Up the Island

The various land units and their associated lore in the Isle of Man make a fascinating study, but it is frustrating because the scholars are politely at loggerheads about the dates and origins of all these units.

Uncertainty begins with the first, basic division of the island into two halves, inaccurately named North and South. They are separated by a borderline running northwest and southwest along the watershed in the central spine of mountains.

The two halves used to regard themselves as virtually separate countries. They were each administered by one of the two deemsters, had their own peculiar laws, and were united only by the national Tynwald. This by tradition was the work of King Godred Crovan after his invasion about 1080. He is said to have settled his followers in the southern half of the island, leaving the northern part as a reservation for the native Manx. The two halves came to blows in 1098, at the Battle of Santwat near Peel, where the North employed women warriors and won, after great slaughter on both sides and the loss of both their leaders. Even today the Manx people claim to perceive a difference between the natives of the northern half, characterized as practical and hardheaded, and the more easygoing southerners.

Godred Crovan became a Manx folk hero, and his legend was interwoven by the old storytellers with episodes in their native mythology. As giant "King Orry," he was generally held responsible for antiquities and customs of unknown origin, but it is unlikely that he or any other Norse ruler was the first to divide the Isle of Man into two halves. The halving of a country, followed by its quartering, was a feature of Celtic ritual, and the north–south division of Man was probably established long before the Norsemen adopted it. Two lawmen or deemsters were therefore required in order to reconcile the Law of Gulating with the traditional Celtic system of administration.

There is evidence, given below, that the two halves of Man were originally subdivided to produce four quarters. As it is, however, each half contains three sheadings. The meaning of this word, the date when these units were introduced, and their original purpose are matters of argument. Some think that "sheading," meaning "a sixth part," represents a Celtic tribal division; others that it was a Norse

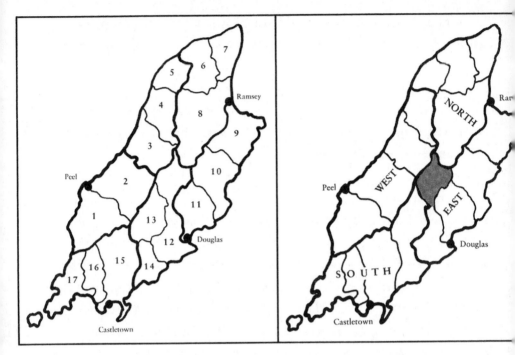

Figure 26a (left). Before recent administrative changes, the parish and sheading divisions of the Isle of Man were as shown in the map and named as follows. In the sheading of Glenfarba, the parishes of (1) Patrick, (2) German. In Michael, (3) Michael, (4) Ballaugh, (5) Jurby. In Ayre, (6) Andreas, (7) Bride, (8) Lezayre. In Garff, (9) Maughold, (10) Lonan, (11) Onchan. In Middle, (12) Braddan, (13) Marown, (14) Santan. In Rushen, (15) Malew, (16) Arbory, (17) Rushen.

Figure 26b (right). This map shows the division of the island into four quarters, which probably preceded the Norse sheading system. The parishes were the same, except that Marown and Santan were originally united as one, giving four parishes to each quarter. The north and west quarters formed the northern division of Man, and the east and south quarters formed the southern division. The four quarter towns were Peel (W), Ramsey (N), Douglas (E), and Castletown (S). The central shaded area, now the northern part of Braddan parish, is bordered by all four quarters and was probably the domain of the Celtic High King of Man.

ship district, implying that it had to provide one ship and its crew for the king's service. With each sheading holding its own Tynwald, the Manx system was parallel to that of Faroe, a similarly sized territory also divided into six Thing districts. It seems likely, therefore, that the six sheadings of Man were a Norse innovation.

Within the sheadings are the parishes. They now number seventeen, but authorities believe that there were once only sixteen parishes, with Marown, the only one with no seacoast, having originally been united with Santan. Again, there is no agreed upon date for when the parishes were formed. Tradition says that the Isle of Man was evangelized by St. Patrick in 447, and that his nephew, St. German, dedicated a chapel in every small settlement. Their contemporary, St. Maughold, grouped these into larger units to institute the parish system.

Parish divisions were not, as this legend implies, made by the early Christians, but existed in pagan times. Many of their boundary lines are evidently prehistoric, and the parochial social structure is also ancient. In Apollonian Greece, a *paroikia* was a district around a temple, the inhabitants of which paid dues to the local priest. In pagan Iceland, the corresponding area was the *godord,* containing twenty or more landed families and with a central temple. Its chief priest was the godi, the senior landowner, and when a Christian minister took over, his district became the *hreppr,* or parish. The Celtic Christians inherited the Druidic system of parishes, each with its lord, priest, and teacher, its main sanctuary, and many lesser shrines.

The sixteen old parishes and the four quarters of the Isle of Man form a coherent system with four parishes to each quarter. The six sheadings break the symmetry by not containing the parishes in equal shares. Of the present seventeen parishes, Glenfarba sheading contains only two, while the others have three each. This supports the likelihood that the sheading divisions were introduced by the Norsemen.

In each Manx parish are a number of farming units called *treens,* and these in turn are divided into four small farms, or quarterlands (in Manx, *kerroo*). Here again is mystery. The great Carl Marstrander, professor of Celtic studies at Oslo University and the author of a history of Man from the Norwegian point of view, concluded, understandably perhaps, that the treen system was introduced by the Vikings. Of the 179 old treen names he collected, most were Norwegian. On the other hand, he wavered, perhaps the uninvited settlers had forced themselves into existing Celtic communities, which were generally organized as three-farm units, and made them into quarterlands by building their own new farmsteads in the center.

The usual size of treens, so Marstrander found, was from 200 to 400 acres. This makes it comparable to the Welsh *trev,* formerly defined as 256 acres. Its fourth part, the *garael,* or allotment of 64 acres, corresponds to the Manx kerroo, and it seems likely, therefore, that the Manx farm units were originally Celtic.

Whatever its origin, the treen formed the basic social unit from at least early Christian times. Marstrander reckoned that every treen once had its *keeill,* a small, simple chapel. About 200 of them are known to have existed in the island. Many have proved to be on pagan sites, near a prehistoric assembly place and holy well. This surely indicates that the treen divisions were instituted in early Celtic times and their boundaries fixed by the symbolic measuring rod of the original kings of Man.

In 1979, the Manx Tynwald officially celebrated its millennium—a thousand years of uninterrupted existence. This prompted a new early history of Man by the Manx and Scandinavian scholar, G. V. C. Young. In *Now Through a Glass Darkly: A History of the Isle of Man under the Norse,* he gave compelling evidence that, after its first division into halves, the island had then been made into four quarters—north, south, east, and west. For a long time, this quartering survived along with the alternative six sheading divisions, and probably it preceded them. The Isle of Man still has its four quarter towns: Castletown, the former capital in the south; Peel, with its sacred island in the west; Ramsey, the Norsemen's harbor in the north; and in the east the modern capital, Douglas. The sixteen parishes were equally divided among the four quarters.

A gruesome relic of the old fourfold division survived into the

Middle Ages, when Manx criminals were sentenced to be hanged and drawn and quartered, and their dismembered parts were sent round for exhibition at each of the four quarter towns.

This division accounts for the different numbers of representatives at different times in the House of Keys. In the heyday of Norwegian colonizing, when the western Scottish islands were under Norse rule, they were divided into four groups and administered together with the Isle of Man as the Kingdom of the Sudreys. The name survives, latinized, in the archaic title of the bishop of Sodor and Mann. The northern Sudreys sent sixteen representatives to the Manx Tynwald, four from each of their four quarters, and the four quarters of Man likewise each contributed their four deputies, one from each parish, sixteen in all. The House of Keys was therefore made up of thirty-two members. When the Mull and Islay groups were ceded to the Scottish chiefs in 1156, their eight members no longer attended, so the number of keys was reduced to twenty-four. It should theoretically have been reduced again, to sixteen, when in 1266 the kings of Man lost the northern group of islands, Lewis and Skye, to the Scots, but the number twenty-four was customary and convenient, so eight other Manx members were appointed to the House of Keys, two from each quarter.

Locating the Center of Man

The division of Man into four provinces is typical of Celtic, Norse, and indeed, ritual landscapes everywhere. Celtic kingdoms also had a fifth, central province set amid the other four. It contained the national sanctuary, administered by the priests and governed under the name of the national deity by the high king. The Irish center, as described in chapter 6, was in Meath, the Middle province. In *Twelve-Tribe Nations,* the authors located the corresponding Welsh sanctuary in the outlying western portion of Radnorshire, "Between Two Rivers."

For hundreds of years, the Manx Tynwald has met on the ancient mound at St. John's, two and one-half miles east of Peel. It is conveniently placed for Al-thing gatherings, but it is not really central in the island. Historians doubt that it was the original Al-thing place. According to Young, "Some people consider that Tynwald was originally held regularly at the hill near St Luke's, and this may well have been so."

It is, in fact, undoubtedly so. With the experience gained from locating other places of national assembly, we can firmly identify the St. Luke's site as the Manx omphalos and former symbolic center.

In the appropriately named sheading of Middle is the parish of Braddan. Its northern part is joined to the rest by a thin neck of land, where the boundary between the two parts of the parish is formed by the river Glass. The northern part, containing St. Luke's in the treen of Balla Christi, is the central precinct of the island, sharing common boundaries with each of the four quarters.

The pole of Man, the line connecting its northernmost and southernmost points, is between Point of Ayre in the far north and Dreswick Point, the southernmost tip of the Langness peninsula. Both points are now marked by lighthouses. On the line between them stands St. Luke's Church.

The natural cross axis of the island is between the two main promontories, which are more or less centrally placed along its northwest and southeast coastlines. The two points are St. Patrick's Island at Peel, the sacred holm with its ancient chapels and cathedral, and Clay Head on the opposite side of the island. The line joining these two points also takes in St. Luke's church, which stands therefore at the intersection of the north–south and east–west axes, at the symbolic center of the Isle of Man.

Dreswick Point is the southernmost tip of the island but not its farthest extremity. The two most widely separated headlands are the northern Point of Ayre and Spanish Head to the southwest. The distance between them is thirty miles. About three hundred yards

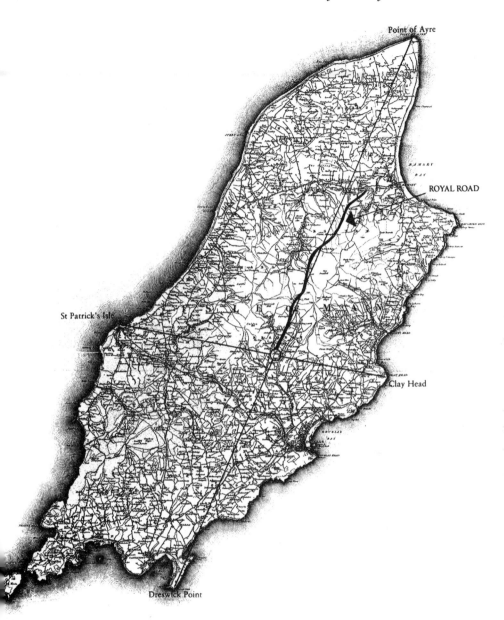

Figure 27. A much-reduced one-inch map of the Isle of Man shows the main axis, between the northernmost and southernmost points of the island, crossing the east–west axis at St. Luke's church at Baldwin, on the site of St. Abban's Chapel near the ancient Tynwald mound. The legendary Royal Road of King Orry runs for two miles on the line of the main axis as it approaches the site.

north of St. Luke's Church is the mound identified as the original Manx Tynwald. The distance from there to Point of Ayre is almost exactly the same as the distance to Spanish Head. If the mound were placed about two hundred yards farther north, it would be precisely equidistant from the two extremities of the Isle of Man. One can try, if one wishes, to explain the slight discrepancy as the effect over centuries of erosion in the southwest and sedimentation in the north of the island. This hardly seems necessary when one visits the site, discovers its history and legends, and appreciates the local conditions that required the church and its Tynwald mound to be placed exactly where they are. One sees then how fitting it is that this magnificent spot should form the center of the central territory of the British Isles.

Approaching the Center:
The Royal Road and the Milky Way

The best way to approach Keeill Abban, the old name for St. Luke's Church, is from the north along the mythological route called the Royal Road. It has now been renamed the Millennium Way and is open as a public footpath across the island.

Two miles north of Keeill Abban, the Royal Road straightens into a formal processional way, aligned precisely on the island's main north–south axis. It runs up to and past the church and the old Tynwald mound behind it, and then makes a slight change of course toward Castletown, the old capital.

The legend of the Royal Road is bound up with that of King Orry, or Gorree, a mysterious ancient ruler whom the Manx regard as their first and best king. The "good old days of King Orry" are looked upon as their golden age. Among his memorials is a long, megalithic, chambered mound in Lonan near the east coast. It is known as the grave of King Orry, implying that he was a giant.

King Orry's first appearance in the Isle of Man is described in a folktale that is possibly derived from the Celtic foundation legend, as told in Train's *Historical Account* of 1845:

> It is reported by oral tradition, that on Gorree's landing at the Laane, on a clear evening, he was met on the beach by a deputation of the inhabitants who had assembled at a distance. One of the deputation demanded whence he came. "That is the way to my country," he replied, pointing to the galaxy or milkyway; and even at the present time this celestial phenomenon is only known to the native Manks as "Raad mooar ree Goree" [the great road of King Gorree, the Royal Road].

The legend of King Orry became attached to Godred Crovan, the Norse king who ruled Man and the Sudreys at the end of the eleventh century. According to the medieval *Chronicle of Mann,* compiled by the monks of Rushen Abbey, he invaded Man with a fleet of small boats that he sailed up the Sulby River from Ramsey. At Milntown, below Sky Hill, he was opposed by an army of Manxmen. By clever military tactics, Godred defeated them and then made a radical departure from custom by sparing their lives, on condition that they confined themselves to the northern half of the island. He ruled well and wisely, codified the laws, and gained the affectionate respect of his Manx subjects.

In both versions of the story, the newly arrived king followed the same route to the center of the realm. He ascended Sky Hill and followed the old Royal Road, which, in the legend, he identified as the Milky Way. This means that it was a sacred path, a processional and pilgrimage road leading to the "pole star" of a central sanctuary. In ancient and early Christian times, the paths to famous pilgrimage centers, such as Walsingham and St. James's Shrine at Santiago, were known as the Milky Way and were seen poetically as reflections of the celestial pathways taken by the gods. Pilgrimage on these ways was a heavenly journey among the stars—the holy shrines along

Figure 28. A painting in the Manx Museum at Douglas shows a proposed statue of King Orry, the legendary Manx ruler. It was designed by the French sculptor Edward Corhould in the 1850s but never executed.

the path—and it was also a mythological journey in the footsteps of the founding gods or saints. At the end of it was the holy center, an image of God's paradise.

The Manx Royal Road, Milky Way, or great road of King Orry should therefore lead toward the central sanctuary of the island. That sanctuary was at Keeill Abban, the central point of the island, about the same distance along the Royal Road from its two ends at Castletown and Ramsey. Here, in the very heart of his realm, we shall find evidence of the lost Celtic High King of Man.

The Sanctuary of the Celtic High King

King Orry's pathway from the north leads downward from mountain land, crosses a ridge, and brings one suddenly to the modern church of St. Luke, with the old Tynwald enclosure behind it. The view from there is magnificent; one can see widely across the southern part of the island and, on a clear day, as far as Anglesey.

St. Luke's is a plain building from 1836, providing a church and schoolhouse for local farms and the nearby small village of Baldwin. Inside it, however, one sees the place with new eyes upon reading a guide sheet by the church warden and historian of the Baldwin district, T. Cowell. He is an elderly scholar whose family has lived and farmed near St. Luke's for many generations, and his writings and memory contain all the traditions about this place that have survived into the twentieth century. From his guide sheet, book of reminiscences (*Baldwin My Valley*), and generous correspondence is drawn the following brief account of Keeill Abban, indicating the supreme significance of this now little-known spot.

The earliest monument at the site is the Tynwald mound, three hundred yards north of the church and alongside the Royal Road. It is not much to look at, a low pile of stones ringed by a modern, protective stone wall. Up to thirty years ago, recalls Cowell, there was a stone at its center, but this with other stones was broken up and carted away by farmers as material for building walls. A notice beside the mound claims it as the "Site of Tynwald, Holden at Killabane 1428." This may have been the last Tynwald "holden" there before it was transferred to St. John's.

The church of St. Luke, on the spot where the north–south axis of the island crosses the east–west line, is most probably on the site of the pagan temple associated with the original Tynwald. Its first Christian dedication was to St. Abban. There was an Irish St. Abban, born in Kildare in the eighth or ninth century, whose ancient tomb in a glen near Ballyvourney, County Cork, flanked with ogham stones, is still venerated. Of the Manx St. Abban, nothing is known apart from his local legend. Like all the early Christians in the Isle of Man, he may well have been an Irishman, but tradition makes him earlier than his namesake of Cork, and he would probably have been buried in the church that he founded and dwelt beside, at Keeill Abban. In March 1992, while St. Luke's was being renovated, builders opened up a crypt below the pulpit and found there an ancient stone coffin with bones. It is quite likely that these were relics of the founder saint, but we shall never know. The coffin was thrown into the rubbish tip, and the bones were decently reinterred in the graveyard.

The local legend is that St. Abban built his simple oratory of sod and stones on the site now occupied by St. Luke's church and lived about a mile north of it, in a little farm called Ulican (Farm of the Saint in Manx). He kept a few animals and poultry and grew crops that he gave to the poor. There was a farm at Ulican until the beginning of this century, when it was drowned by the new reservoir at Injebreck.

The oratory was soon replaced by a stone keeill, the ruins of which survived up to 1836, when Bishop Ward built his church there. A few of the old keeill stones were incorporated in the new building, including a square block of red sandstone with a cross carved into one face, which was given a place of honor in the outside, east wall of the church, below the belfry. This stone is known locally as the Cursed Stone of Destiny, but it should rather be called a cursing stone, as its story, told by Cowell in his guide sheet, suggests.

A certain farmer, living nearby at Algare Farm, wished to build a new cow shed and removed some stones which included the incised

Figure 29. St. Luke's church, rebuilt in 1836 on the site of St. Abban's Oratory.

cross stone from the ruins of the then ancient keeill. After he had built the new cow shed, things began to go all wrong for him on the farm. All his animals became sick and died, his sheep, cows, pigs, horses and finally his wife fell ill. He became so afraid that she too would die, that he pulled down the cow shed with all haste. She survived and in thankfulness for his wife's complete recovery to health once more, he set about with gusto to help Bishop Ward to rebuild the new church in 1836.

By ancient tradition this place is a holy sanctuary. "St Luke's Church door is never locked, as a murderer fleeing from his victim's relatives can still seek refuge and shelter in it."

A stone of destiny is a Celtic coronation stone, and there is no harm in supposing that the block in the wall at St. Luke's was the stone on which the old Manx kings were installed. Whether or not this was so, the place retains other royal associations. To the east, it is flanked by a high ridge that still has the Celtic name, Slieu Ree, or the King's Mountain. If the Manx king, seated beside the central stone on the Tynwald mound, had looked to the east, as is the custom today at St. John's Tynwald, he would have faced this mountain across the Royal Road.

Yet at this site, the eye is inevitably drawn to look down its axis toward the south, and anyone who goes there will recognize that the king upon the mound must have turned his face in that direction and toward St. Abban's Keeill. According to Prudence Jones, an authority on pagan Nordic ritual, kings and judges sat at the north end of an axis and were formally approached from the south. This, she believes, was the original orientation of the St. John's Tynwald, reflecting the design of the Thing on Yngling Hill in Sweden. Ritually installed, the old king of Ireland sat facing south, and so

Figure 30. A stone for a king's foot. Every Celtic tribe had its stone of installation, sometimes carved with a footprint. Only a few remain, but this stone, found at Castleward mound (probably a local Tynwald site) in the Isle of Man, is likely to be a relic of Manx Celtic royalty.

did the old emperor of China. The custom of facing east arose later, perhaps due to Christian influence. At Keeill Abban, the archaic orientation is perpetuated by the natural design of the site, emphasized by the north–south alignment of the Tynwald mound and the former keeill.

In agreement with this identification of Keeill Abban as a Celtic royal sanctuary, Cowell writes: "All around Keeill Abban we have royal connections—paths, little farms now under the Reservoir, Slieu Ree the king hill, Algare Farm (meaning Hill of Law) near St Luke's parsonage. On old Tynwald hill just behind St Luke's all the Manx laws were promulgated up to 1428 and murderers could seek justice. We also have other Tynwald hills around the island but not like Keeil Abban's."

Even those who are quite unaware of Keeill Abban's historical significance are impressed by the spiritual atmosphere of the place. This and the symbolic features of the surrounding landscape befit it perfectly as the royal ceremonial center. The church and Tynwald stand upon a narrow spur of land sloping down southward from the central mountains. To the east and west, it is bordered by rivers in deep valleys, and beyond these are the two protecting ridges of Slieu Ree and the Creg Hill. To the north stands the pyramid-shaped mountain of Carraghan, the symbolic guardian. The Tynwald is evidently sited in relation to it, for as one reaches the mound, approaching it from the church, the mountain's peak starts to become visible, rising up over a ridge. Strange tales about Carraghan and its haunted slopes are recorded in Manx folklore. A bonfire would have blazed upon its summit, with others lit upon the hills to east and west, while the old Tynwald was in session.

At this site, with Carraghan at one's back and long, high ridges to left and right, one has the feeling of being enthroned—sheltered and secluded while gazing over hundreds of little fields as far as the southern headlands. Upon seeing this place, one can hardly doubt

Figure 31. Looking southward over St. Luke's Church from the Tynwald mound at Keeill Abban, one can share the impressive view once enjoyed by the old Manx king. If this photograph had been taken on a clear day instead of in the normal Manx mist, it would show hundreds of little fields across the southern part of the island and include a distant view of Anglesey.

that this was where the Celtic king presided over the original Manx Tynwald.

There are records to show that the Tynwald was sometimes held elsewhere, at Reneurling near the Church of Kirk Michael and at the gates of Castle Rushen, the seat of kings and governors from the twelfth century. These were probably the sites of local Things. The present meeting place at St. John's is very old, certainly prehistoric. Its Tynwald hill and adjoining keeill were once enclosed by ditches and earthworks, entered through stone archways that were compared to those of Stonehenge. All these antiquities were swept away in

Figure 32. As one approaches the old Tynwald mound, walking northward from St. Luke's Church, the central mountain, Carraghan, rises suddenly into view. Here, it is just beginning to appear over the ridge.

1849, when the keeill was rebuilt as St. John's Church and the area around it made smooth and tidy. Young suggests that the national Tynwald was moved there at the end of the eleventh century, when King Magnus Barelegs of Norway built the castle on the island at Peel in place of the former monastery. Peel was his residence and the center of Norse rule, so the St. John's site would have served his convenience better than the more distant Keeill Abban. It appears that St. John's was originally an important regional Tynwald. It lies on the direct line between the northern tip of the island, Point of Ayre, and the south end of its northern division, the high cliff at Braddan Head. An alternative cross axis, from Peel to Douglas Head, also passes through the site. This may indicate that St. John's was originally the Tynwald for the northern division of the Isle of Man.

The celebration in 1979 of the thousand-year-old Tynwald at St. John's did not greatly impress the churchpeople at Keeill Abban. After all, the newly named Millennium Way passes not by St. John's, but through their sanctuary, which they know be the ancient center of the island. In talking to them about this, one has the impression that they quietly regard the St. John's Tynwald as a rather recent upstart.

Inside the Royal Precinct

The axis lines identified in these studies are not to be confused with "leys" or straight alignments of ancient sites, previously referred to in connection with the Cornish ceremonial center, the Boscawen-un stone circle. Oriented toward the rising and setting points on the horizon of the sun, moon, and certain stars, they converge upon megalithic centers and must somehow have contributed to their ritual purpose. The stone alignments to and from Boscawen-un and other circles possibly denoted symbolic or actual boundaries, and no doubt they had much further significance in tribal lore. But that is another story. Leys and megalithic alignments are generally confined to a limited area, reflecting the local rather than national organization of Neolithic farming societies.

The geographical axes that concern us here evidently belong to later, Bronze Age times, when whole countries were united, symbolically at least, by the institution of sacred kingship. From the central point, located on the world-pole, a solar-zodiacal pattern was laid across the realm, incorporating the ancient sanctuaries together with many of the archaic land divisions and customs based upon them, within a large-scale geographical design. The extensive axes that locate the symbolic centers of Celtic and Norse kingdoms seem quite unconnected with megalithic sites and alignments.

At Keeill Abban, however, there is a short and very remarkable line of sites, passing through St. Luke's Church, that has the hall-marks of antiquity. Without knowing how to place or date it, one can only observe the fact of its existence before leaving it aside for future study.

This alignment is between the four quarterland farms, together with the church, in the treen of Balla Christi. The Manorial Roll of the Isle of Man, a list of land holdings for the years 111 to 1515, records that in this treen are the quarterlands of Ulican, Algare, Ballamodda, and Renscault. These farms are still there today, apart from Ulican, which was submerged almost a hundred years ago by the reservoir. Earlier maps show its site together with the others.

All these places lie precisely on one straight line less than two miles long. From the north downward the order is: Ulican, St. Luke's Church, Algare, Ballamodda, and Renscault. Between Ulican and the church is a small farm, or croft, with the Manx name, Lhergy Awhallan. This, too, is on the alignment. Thus the four quarterland farms, together with another farm and the church—six sites in all—were placed (or occur by chance?) on a short straight line. This line forms the polar axis for the northern part of Braddan Parish, extending from its northern head to its southern foot and dividing it into two virtually equal halves.

It is significant that the central treen of Man was named Balla Christi and dedicated in early Christian times to the supreme lord of the new faith. This is likely to have perpetuated a previous pagan dedication to the supreme Celtic deity. It implies that this treen, this central area bordered by each of the four quarters of Man, was a sacred, Druidic precinct, dedicated to the god, whose representative was the high king. At the northern end of this area, a thin neck of land, bordered by streams, ends in the wooded valley named Druid Dale. It is said, though without positive evidence, that the name is not ancient, but it is certainly appropriate to this beautiful, secluded spot. It could well have been the most sacred grove of the Manx Druids. This place has also been submerged by a modern reservoir.

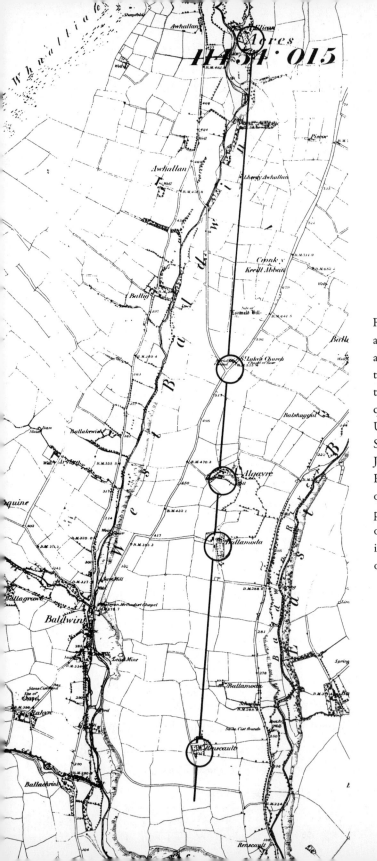

Figure 33. St. Luke's church and the Tynwald mound at Keeill Abban are in the treen of Balla Christi. The treen is made up of four quarterland farmsteads: Ulican (the Farm of the Saint), Algare (the Hill of Justice), Ballamodda, and Renscault. These four stand on a straight alignment that passes through the center of each farmstead and also includes St. Luke's church on the site of Keeill Abban.

The traditional story of St. Abban, recorded by Cowell, has a certain association with the alignment of Balla Christi's church and farms. From Ulican, the Farm of the Saint, he would walk to his oratory on the site of the present church. Thus, he would have trodden the northern part of the alignment. There is now no visible path on that line, but Cowell tells of other traditional pathways that converge on the church, including the Corpse Track, on which coffins were carried through West Baldwin. Apart from their legends, there is now little to denote these old pathways.

The plan of this sacred area between the four quarters of Man shows two extensions, north and south, which emphasize its axis. Both these arms are enclosed on three sides by streams, symbolically insulating the central realm. Its borders are defined by springs, from which streams and rivers flow north, south, east, and west to every part of the island. The four main rivers of Man have their sources there. They are the Neb, which flows west to Peel; the Sulby, going north to Ramsey; and Awin Glass (Bright River) and Awin Dhoo (Dark River), which together provide the name for the coastal town, Douglas, where they meet in the southeast.

Rarely could there be found such a place as this center of the Isle of Man. Nature has almost perfectly adapted it to supply all the symbolic and mythological requirements of a sacred precinct, reflecting the traditional image of paradise. In view of its outstanding qualities, it may not be implausible to attribute to this sanctuary two different levels of significance. The first, obviously, is that here was the sacred domain of the Celtic King of Man. One should also consider the ancient reputation of the Isle of Man as a center of the Druidic mysteries, as well as its geographical position as the natural omphalos of the British Isles. The conclusion to which this is pointing is that the Tynwald mound at Keeill Abban was not merely the Manx ceremonial center, but was also once venerated as the inner sanctum for an entire religious system, the religion of Druidry throughout Britain and Ireland.

5

A DIVERSION TO THE CENTER
OF ENGLAND

Calculations on the Geographical Center

In the village of Meriden, Warwickshire, between Birmingham and Coventry, stands an old stone cross that traditionally marks the very center of England. It is a striking claim, and many people seem to have heard of it, but no one knows when it arose or with what justification.

Where is the center of England, or mainland Britain, or the British Isles? Some scientific answers were provided in 1941 by Sir Charles Arden-Close, director general of the Ordnance Survey, which were published in *The Geographical Journal*. His definition of the center point of any country (assuming the earth to be a sphere) was "that point through which any great circle will divide the country into two parts of equal moment." He then gave the procedure for discovering the geographical center of England.

The usual way of finding the centre of a country is to cut out, in cardboard, or in thin metal, an outline of the country, and to suspend this outline map on a vertical surface from various points on its perimeter, and then to draw vertical lines through the points of suspension. The point where these vertical lines intersect will be the required centre. Or, instead of drawing vertical lines from each point of suspension, a vertical line may be drawn, once and for all, on the vertical wall or surface, and its intersections with the perimeter marked. In this case it may be well to reverse the outline-map and carry out the same process on the back, so as to eliminate the effect of any error in the supposed vertical line.

In looking for his centers, first of England and Wales together and then of England alone, Arden-Close acknowledged two traditional claimants, both in Warwickshire: the cross at Meriden and an ancient tree, the Lillington Oak, at Leamington. Neither of these places was indicated by his suspended map. His center of England alone was "on Watling Street, 4 miles ESE of Atherstone, close to the railway bridge, between the villages of Higham-on-the-Hill and Caldecote." For England and Wales together, "the point is about 2 miles NNE of Castle Bromwich, about 3 miles south-east of Sutton Coldfleld, and 7 miles north-east of the centre of Birmingham." Both centers are in Warwickshire, about ten miles from Meriden and twenty miles from Leamington.

These secular, geographical centers have no historical significance and are of merely academic interest. They do, however, support the tradition that the center of England is somewhere in Warwickshire.

England's Natural Axis

In the preceding chapter on the Isle of Man, the main axis of the British Isles was identified as the line between the northeast and southwest extremities, Duncansby Head beyond John o' Groats in Scotland and the Land's End of Cornwall. Mainland Britain also has an obvious pole or north–south axis. From Duncansby Head, it passes through the middle of England to St. Catherine's Point at the southern tip of the Isle of Wight. There are several headlands on the central southern coast of England that are dedicated to St. Catherine, who is, among other things, the patron of both philosophers and

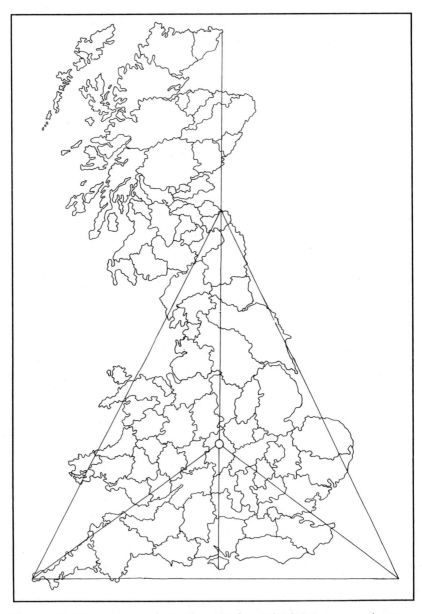

Figure 34. The main north–south axis of mainland Britain runs between Duncansby Head and St. Catherine's Point. It crosses the coast of southern Scotland at the point where the former Scottish county, Haddingtonshire, joins Berwickshire. This was once the most northern point of England. Equidistant from that point and the opposite extremity at the Land's End, Meriden stands on the main axis, at the center of an isosceles triangle, and is thus suitably placed to be regarded as the center of England.

weavers. This suggests that the main axis, resting as it were on St. Catherine's lap, was once imagined as a spindle, Plato's image of the world-pole.

On its course from the northeast tip of Scotland, southward over the Firth of Forth, the axis line regains the coast at the point that separates the old counties of Haddingtonshire (now East Lothian) and Berwickshire. At the beginning of history, Berwickshire belonged to the Saxon kingdom of Northumbria, and its border with Haddingtonshire was the original border between England and Scotland. The terminus point of that border, on the east coast, would then have been the most northern spot in England. From that spot to St. Catherine's Point, the line forms the natural axis of England and Wales together, dividing the country into two roughly equal portions.

On or very near that axis line stands the ancient cross at Meriden, which traditionally marks the very center of England. Emphasizing this claim is the fact that Meriden is virtually equidistant from the northern point of the axis, at the onetime border with Scotland, and the southwest tip of Cornwall. An isosceles triangle (figure 34) centered on the main axis, with its apex on the old Scottish border and containing almost the whole of England and Wales, has Meriden at its center.

Meriden

At first sight, there is nothing remarkable about Meriden. It is a straggling village, much expanded by new houses since the 1960s, in the small area of country that survives between industrial Birmingham and Coventry in Warwickshire. The strangest thing about it is its legendary reputation as the midpoint of England. No one knows how or when this legend arose. The early topographical writers make no mention of it, but the belief has long been established locally and is widely known throughout England today.

MERIDEN CROSS—The Centre of England.   SIDWELL, MERID

Figure 35. Postcards from the beginning of the twentieth century popularized the reputation of Meriden Cross in Warwickshire as the central point of England. Bicyclist clubs adopted it as their rallying place.

From a search through old books of Warwickshire lore, it appears that the first reference to Meriden as the center was written in 1876 by J. Tom Burgess, author of *Historic Warwickshire*. He also mentions a rival center about twelve miles away in Leamington Spa.

Amongst the folk lore of Warwickshire there is a widespread idea, not only that the county is the centre of England, but different localities are specially distinguished. Near Leamington, on the Lillington road, there is an oak tree standing by the side of the road on an elevated mound, which is universally called the centre of England. At Meriden, the cross there is stated to be the exact spot, though it has been moved in the memory of man.

The moving of the Meriden Cross took place about two hundred years ago. Its original site is not exactly known, but it was near where it now stands, on the green at the village center. In 1952, it was moved again, but only a few yards. According to Doreen Agutter's local history, its capstone, now lost, took the form of a Doric capital, so evidently it was more like a central pillar than a specifically Christian monument. It may be that Warwickshire folklore preserved its original significance as the central pillar of England.

Meriden is supposed to mean "miry valley," but it is suggestive coincidence that the name occurs on the "meridian" through the center of England. It could even possibly have derived from Mediolanum, the Roman-Celtic name for the central city. Previous to the thirteenth century, when the name was first recorded, Meriden was known as Alspath, another interesting word for place-name enthusiasts. In times before the encroachments of industry, it lay secluded in the ancient Forest of Arden, where, at the heart of England, Shakespeare set *As You Like It.* This was a legendary haunt of Robin Hood, native spirit of the wildwoods, who was said to have taken part in archery contests in the forest. "Robin Hood's horn" is still preserved at Meriden, in the headquarters of the Woodmen of Arden, the oldest and most exclusive archery society in Britain, known to have existed long before its formal constitution in 1785. Its eighty members, in their archaic dress of green hat and coat, white trousers, and buff waistcoat with brass buttons of the society, hold summer "Wardmotes," or shooting matches, with yew bows and locally made arrows. Most of their ritual dates from the eighteenth century, but their precious relics and mysterious origins hint at earlier traditions of summer festival. The old association of Meriden with its venerable horn is suggested by some of the parish place-names, including Horn Brook, Horn Pond, Hornwood, Cornet's End (from *cornu,* or horn), and Blowhorn Lane.

From the beginning of the twentieth century, Meriden's local fame grew to become national. Postcards were printed showing its cross as the country's central pivot, and in 1921, the Wheelmen of England erected their own Centre of England monument on Meriden Green. It is a concrete pillar in memory of bicyclists killed in the First, and now the Second, World War. Cyclists from all over England converge on it each year on May 24, when an open-air service is held there.

Nor is this the only alternative center at Meriden. In the old village inn, the Bull's Head, a brass plaque on the floor, symbolically inscribed with an eye, target, and crossed arrows, claims to mark the midpoint of England. It was made from a shell case by Italian prisoners of war in the 1940s.

The Center of Roman Britain

The northern boundary of early Roman Britain was marked by Hadrian's Wall, with its eastern terminus at the mouth of the river Tyne. From a fort at that spot, the line to St. Catherine's Point in the far south formed at that time the main axis of the country, and upon it the Roman surveyors located the official centerpoint of Britain. Their monumental High Cross at Venonae stood at the crossing of two great roads, Watling Street from London and the southeast into north Wales, and the Fosse Way from south Devon to Lincoln.

The site of High Cross, five miles southeast of Hinckley in Leicestershire, is on the county boundary with Warwickshire, where four parishes have their meeting point. It was once a beacon site and commands such wide views that, according to Burgess's *Historic Warwickshire,* "fifty-seven churches may be seen from the spot without help of a glass." Its reputation as the center of England long survived the Roman monument, and in 1711, the justices of Warwickshire ordered a new marker to be erected there, both to honor the old center and to guide travelers on the Fosse Way and Watling Street. At a cost of £400, the self-styled "noblemen and gentry, ornaments of the neighbouring counties of Warwick and Leicester" set up a tall pillar with a Latin inscription beginning, in translation, "If, O traveller, you are in quest of the footsteps of the ancient Romans, here you may behold them. Here their once most famous military roads cross one another and extend to the farthest limits of Britain."

The ruins of the pillar, standing on an ancient tumulus, were still to be seen in the last quarter of the nineteenth century. Nothing

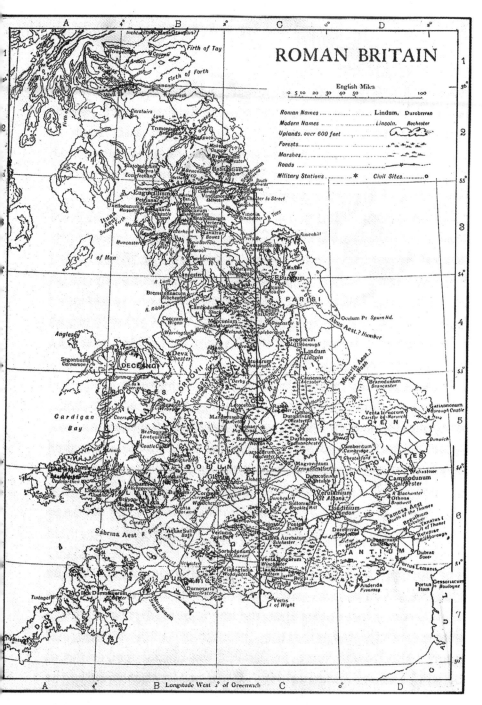

Figure 36. The eastern bastion at South Shields of Hadrian's fortified wall marked the northernmost point of early Roman Britain. From there to St. Catherine's Point, Isle of Wight, ran the main axis of the country, passing through the Roman center at High Cross (Venonae).

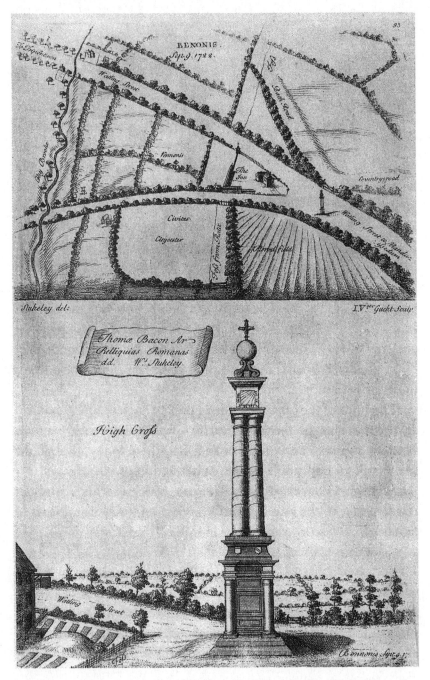

Figure 37. William Stukeley's drawings of 1724 show the High Cross, the center of Roman Britain, and a bird's-eye view of its site on the border between Leicestershire and Warwickshire, where Watling Street crosses the Fosse Way.

much of antiquity can be found there today, though the site is still an important center, as a junction of motorways.

At High Cross, the Roman axis on which it stands is about twelve miles to the east of the Meriden cross on the "natural" axis of Britain.

Rival Centers

Before joining in the popular acclaim of Meriden as the omphalos of England, it is fair to examine the claims made on behalf of rivals. Firmly supported by local partisans is the Midland Oak at Lillington, on the western outskirts of Leamington. According to a recent book on old Leamington, its claim to be the central pillar of England goes back no less than eight centuries.

Deprived during the Second World War of the railings that once protected it, the Midland Oak died, and its relics were soon afterward

Figure 38. The Midland Oak at Lillington, near Leamington Spa, Warwickshire, is the main rival to Meriden Cross as the central pillar of England. The claim is affirmed on a brass plaque beside the recently planted sapling on the site of the old oak.

removed. Traditional tree sites, however, are more lasting than any individual specimen, and in 1982, a new oak, a sapling from the original stock, was ceremonially planted on the correct spot. In front of it, a stone bears a plaque commemorating the event and reaffirming the status of the Midland Oak as England's true center. Leamington people refer scornfully to the pretensions of Meriden.

This whole subject, neglected for many years, seems recently to have become topical, and several previously unheard of "centers of England" now have their partisans. In his booklet, *The Quest for the Omphalos*, Bob Trubshaw lists various places that have been suggested, including Oxford, Lichfield in Staffordshire, Croft Hill in Leicestershire, and important road junctions at Dunstable and Royston. John Walbridge contributes the statement that "the geographical omphalos of England lies in Northamptonshire, just south of Daventry," which is the part of England most distant from the sea. He identifies the spot as Arbury Hill, where the territories of three Celtic tribes converged.

Writing about the omphalos in *The Ancient Science of Geomancy*, Nigel Pennick notes that in the time of Bede, the ninth century, Lichfield was considered to be the center of England. The "staple," or cross shaft, at Dunstable, where Watling Street crosses the Icknield Way, may have had a similar reputation, and at Royston, Hertfordshire, is Pennick's "perfect geomantic centre" on the crossing of the Icknield Way and Ermine Street. The spot is marked by an omphalos rock, the King Stone, and below it a subterranean chamber, carved with archaic figures emblematic of the "mysteries," was discovered in 1742.

The rise of Oxford to become England's main center of learning begins with its traditional foundation by the Celtic king Lludd. A story in *The Mabinogion* tells how he was instructed to measure the length and breadth of England in order to determine its center. At that spot, he would find two fighting dragons that were responsible for the evils afflicting the nation. They were discovered at Oxford. This typifies the combination of land surveying and divination in traditional augury or geomancy.

Some of these places are by no means central within the present boundaries of England, and their former significance was evidently regional rather than national. Boundaries change and land units are constantly regrouped, so it is never easy to identify the original center of any local inland district. Yet even on the parochial scale, there is evidence that the local place of assembly was sited, as far as possible, at the geographical center. There is an example of this in Vaughan Cornish's monograph, *Historic Thorn Trees in the British Isles.* At Salcombe Regis in south Devon, a succession of thorn trees has marked the traditional spot where open-air manor courts were held. Cornish was struck by the central position of this site and found, when he examined it on a map, that "the diagonal lines connecting the four corners of the ancient parish intersect at the point where the Thorn Tree stands."

Returning to the question of the national omphalos, the conclusion indicated by tradition and the facts of geography is that Meriden Cross, located on the island's main axis and equidistant from Land's End and the northernmost point on the ancient border with Scotland, is most fittingly regarded as the center of England.

A Cornish Center in West Penwith

A corner of the British Isles that is almost an island, with a tradition of independent rule under a Celtic king, is the far western promontory of Cornwall, in the district of West Penwith, terminating at the Land's End. Its eastern boundary is between Hayle and St. Michael's Mount, where a low, watery neck of land joins it to the rest of the county.

The southwestern Celtic kingdom of Dumnonia once extended from Cornwall as far as Somerset, but from the fifth century, its eastern territories were gradually lost to the Saxons. Finally, in 927, the Saxon Athelstan defeated the last Cornish king, Howell, the Celtic name for the sun, in a battle traditionally held near a stone circle, the Merry Maidens, in the far west of Cornwall.

The fourteen old parishes west of St. Michael's Mount are famous among archaeologists for their great collection of prehistoric and early Christian monuments, indicating the ancient, sacred character of the district. It was the last stronghold of Cornish independence and culture, the native language survived there into the eighteenth century, and even now it is perceptibly different from the rest of Cornwall. This old sanctuary would undoubtedly have had its ritual center. The site has long been forgotten, but it is likely to have been situated by the principles of ritual geography, in the very center and on the main axis of the district.

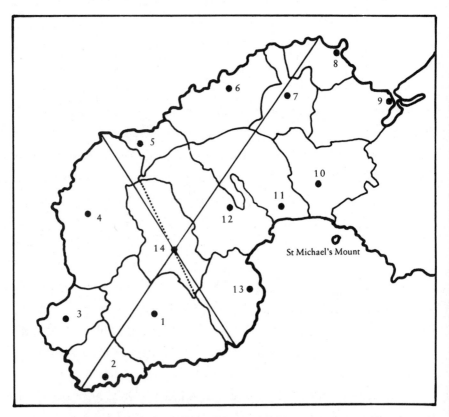

Figure 39. The old parishes of West Penwith are (1) St. Buryan, (2) St. Levan, (3) Sennen, (4) St. Just, (5) Morvah, (6) Zennor, (7) Towednack, (8) St. Ives, (9) Lelant, (10) Ludgvan, (11) Gulval, (12) Madron, (13) Paul, and (14) Sancreed. Only Sancreed has no access to the sea. The main axis from the north to the south of the district meets the cross axis at Sancreed church.

The main axis of West Penwith, dividing it into two halves, is between its northernmost headland, Clodgy Point, and its south-western extremity, Gwennap Head. The longest diagonal to this line runs between the northwest and southeast corners of West Penwith, at Pendeen Head and Carn-du near Lamorna. These two diagonals intersect beside the old church at Sancreed.

Sancreed is the central parish of West Penwith, the only one that is entirely inland with no border on the sea. Its dedication is mysterious. There is no record of a St. Creed, and the old local pronunciation, "san-crist," has been taken to imply that the original dedication was to Jesus Christ. This suggests a comparison between Sancreed Parish and the corresponding central area of the Isle of Man, the treen of Balla Christi, which contains Keeill Abban and the original Tynwald site. Like St. Luke's church on the site of Keeill Abban, Sancreed Church stands on the main axis of its parish, from the southernmost point to the meeting of boundaries on its northern edge.

There is not even a village at Sancreed today, just the church, a farm, and a few nearby houses, but the network of old tracks and paths that converge on it from all quarters indicate that it was once an important place of ritual assembly. The quaint old church, with foundations from the thirteenth century, is built on a raised mound, and its circular churchyard signifies that it was a Celtic *llan,* or sacred enclosure, probably of pagan origin. Within the parish around it are many relics of the ancient religion, stone pillars, holy wells, hilltop earthworks, and prehistoric settlements. The rock-chambered holy well opposite the church has been called "the most atmospheric in Cornwall."

In the church are remnants of a curiously carved old screen with figures of forgotten symbolism, including a crowned head with three faces, perhaps a memory of the former Celtic king. Standing in the churchyard are several old stone crosses. One of them, nine feet long, is among the finest of its kind in Cornwall. On three of its four sides, at the top of the shaft below the head, is a design almost unknown

Figure 40. In front of Sancreed church stands a Celtic cross with, below the head, the crossing of diagonal lines, perhaps a reference to the axis lines that meet there.

elsewhere, a plain rectangle with its two diagonals forming a cross. There is no better explanation for this than that it represents the four lines from the four quarters of West Penwith meeting at Sancreed.

At this beautiful, secluded spot, the imagination is easily stirred. Anyone who goes there will see how appropriately this geographical center might also have formed the sacred ritual center of the far Western kingdom.

6

THE CENTER OF IRELAND

Myths of Foundation

The center of Ireland today is just a spot on the ground, but in ancient times it was the heart and pivot of an elaborately structured, ritualized kingdom, built on a foundation plan that was held to represent the ideal order of the universe. A relic of those times and that form of society is the Irish tradition of music, learning, poetry, and fine speech. Even today, the level of Irish popular culture remains higher than in neighboring lands, and in mythology, genealogy, archaeology, and records of ancient lore, Ireland is far richer than any other country of northern Europe. As everywhere else, Ireland's traditional culture is under fierce attack by the television-diffused influences of modernism, but a culture so ancient and deep-rooted, so closely related to the native spirit of the land and people, will not easily be eradicated. The fact is, however, that the old myths, legends, customs, games, and music have lost their original functions, are no longer essential to daily life, and are now preserved mainly by scholars or those who happen to care for such things. Modern "Celtic revivals" have been attempted, but with narrow success, and it is now evident that the only possible revival of culture is from the heart—not just the emotional heart, but the very core of that traditional code of wisdom that was instituted in the cosmological order of ancient Ireland.

This whole inquiry into ritual centers is mainly on a geographical, antiquarian level, but it also has practical, personal value in that these centers are symbols of an ideally governed state and have a correspondingly harmonious effect on minds. In the case of Ireland, the symbol of the national, unifying center is particularly powerful, both as a reminder of the ancient tradition and as an image that transcends modern religious and political divisions.

From early Christian times, historians have tried to compile the definitive history of Ireland, selecting items from bardic lore to illustrate a certain sequence of events. Many fine narratives have been produced, but their historical value is negated by the nature of their sources, which are mythological and describe cyclical rather than linear processes. Moreover, there is not just one mythological cycle but many, each relating to a certain period and part of the country, yet with age-old, universal themes.

The old chroniclers wove their stories around a series of invasions, beginning in about 3000 BC with Caesair, whom Christian writers identified as a daughter of Noah. With fifty women and three men, she populated Ireland at the time of the Flood. Two other invasions followed, those of Partholón and Nemed, whose adventures are set out in the great Irish epic, the *Lebor Gabála* (*Book of Invasions*), and then came the Fir Bolg, worshippers of the lightning god, Bolga. They were succeeded by the Tuatha dé Danaan, a magical race who in some accounts arrived through the air. The final invasion was that of the Milesians, the Sons of Mil, who came from Spain during the first millennium BC and are the legendary ancestors of the Celts.

Having defeated the Tuatha dé Danaan, the Milesians drove them underground, into the *raths* and mounds, where they merged with the fairy folk. Also dispossessed were the monstrous Fomorians, a race of elemental giants whose legends hint at their probable origin as archaic deities of the early megalith builders. At each successive invasion, the newcomers formed a higher caste above their predecessors while assimilating their magical traditions. Continuity was provided by the goddess, the eternal spirit of Ireland, whose favors had to be won by every invader before the new settlement was permitted. As Ériu, or Éire, queen-goddess of the Tuatha dé Danaan, she saw the landing of the Sons of Mil, and with her two sisters made a bargain with them, granting them lawful occupation of the island on condition that they called it by the sisters' three names—Éire, Banba, and Fódla.

The traditional list of Irish sovereigns, compiled from bardic records, claims a succession of 189 high kings, beginning in remote antiquity with Sláinge the Fir Bolg and ending in 1175 when the last Irish king, Roderick O'Connor, paid homage to Henry II of England. It names nine Fir Bolg and nine Tuatha dé Danaan rulers, followed by eighty-nine Milesians up to the year AD 1. Modern historians attach no significance to the early records, but the old scholars took them more seriously, being aware of the bardic disciplines, strictly enforced in the Druidic colleges, that limited the recitation of genealogies to carefully educated, professional storytellers. Before its dilution with Christian themes and the disruptions caused by Viking and later invaders, the continuity of oral tradition preserved memories from probably as far back as the Bronze Age. The character and adventures of the old kings are legendary, but the antiquity of their line is undoubted, and the 107 High Kings listed before the birth of Christ may not greatly exceed the actual number of prehistoric national rulers. The average recorded length of each reign is about twenty years, making the date of the first King of Ireland about 2000 BC, the approximate date of Stonehenge and, according to some modern scholars, of the beginnings of Celtic culture in the British Isles.

Kings and Constitution

From about AD 300, Irish history begins to emerge from the mists of mythology and provides glimpses of a prosperous, populous, high-spirited nation, consisting of many different tribes and people, administered by an array of chiefs, princes, kings, and Druids, with a Metropolitan Druid and the High King of all Ireland as supreme authorities. Two contrasting elements, stability and change, were ever-present in this constitution. Everyone's rights, duties, and position in society were defined by strict, detailed codes of law, yet within the hierarchy was constant flux as local rulers lost or added to their possessions and families rose and descended in prescribed order, up and down the social scale. The effect was of a constant interplay between order and chaos, the preordained and the incidental, which is typical of the universe itself.

Some of the earliest Irish documents are books of law. They specify exactly what is due to whom, from whom, and on what occasion. The qualifications for each of the many grades of society are laid down in terms of land and livestock, and each level of landholder is instructed on the rents and taxes he may levy, when, where, in what circumstances he may collect them, and the gifts he is expected to offer in return. Seven classes of chieftain were recognized. The lowest, the *aire désa,* had to have at least seven tenant smallholders, twelve cows, sixteen sheep, a grain-drying kiln, a mill, and a barn. His minimum landholding was at least fourteen cumals, a cumal being equal in value to a servant woman or three cows. At the other extreme was the king. As with all other ranks, the kings were distinguished by different grades according to their possessions. Most ordinary was the *ri,* the ruler of a small *tuath,* or kingdom. Above him was the *ri ruirech,* ruling several *tuatha* together; then came the provincial kings, four of whom paid tribute to the High King of Ireland.

Corresponding to this political hierarchy were those of the Druid priests—later the clergy—and the *filid,* the professional, educated class of clerks, lawyers, teachers, and masters of the secular arts. Their highest representative was the *ollamh,* the professor, who ranked equal with a king or a bishop. In the same way, the different grades of ruler, priest, and scholar associated with each other on the appropri-

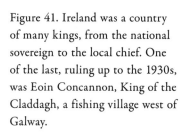

Figure 41. Ireland was a country of many kings, from the national sovereign to the local chief. One of the last, ruling up to the 1930s, was Eoin Concannon, King of the Claddagh, a fishing village west of Galway.

ate level, forming at the most humble end of the scale the trinity of squire–vicar–village schoolmaster that Oliver Goldsmith (an Irishman from Country Westmeath) glorified in *The Deserted Village*.

This peaceful, ordered prospect is only one side of the picture. The chiefs and their followers were vigorous young men, impelled by their natures and their entire upbringing to emulate the heroic deeds of their ancestors. Their main occupations were hunting game and raiding their neighbors, and they were ever ready to profit from the weakness or sleepiness of rivals. Competition among them was relentless, though generally, one can suppose, good-humored. Grievances were small, local, and quickly worked out. While clans and families gained and lost influence, everything took place within the same stable, traditional social order, which imitated the order of the cosmos.

Kings and chiefs were only partly hereditary. At any time, certain families only were eligible for election to kingship, but these constantly changed as power or popular acclaim brought new candidates into office, while previously eligible families succumbed to the four-generation rule. This rule was that, if within four generations, from great-grandfather to great-grandson, a member of the family had not been elected king, that family fell in rank and was no longer qualified.

The effect of this was to promote an energetic, ever-changing aristocracy, vying with each other for the privilege of leading their people; and this was a very practical arrangement, for it was in everyone's interest that the chief should be strong, active, and imaginative, should uphold justice, attract favorable weather, and defeat all enemies. At every level, kings and chiefs were elected at open assembly by their peers. Everyone knew whom they were voting for and why they were voting for him. It was necessary to choose the very best man among them, the man whom the goddess of their country would willingly accept at the ceremony of his installation, whom she would favor with her gifts, thus benefiting all his dependants.

Throughout every period of history, Ireland has been the lawful, acknowledged possession of her native goddess, who preceded all invasions. Kings and chiefs came and went, and she was bride to them all. Those she did not like were rejected and fell from power. She did not always follow the conventional morality, sometimes choosing a strong lover from a lowly, unqualified family, but she was a firm upholder of culture and custom, a lady who would not be satisfied with an uncouth boor but demanded the best educated, the most courteous, charming, brave, and handsome young man of the district. A feature of Celtic coronations, and of such ceremonies all over the ancient world, was the ritual wedding of the new king to the eternal goddess. She had different names, tastes, and attributes in different parts of the country, and her ways and whims were never quite predictable. Yet even today she is Queen of Ireland, the Virgin Mary worshipped in a thousand grottoes, while Christ the King, a popular figure in Irish religious imagery, corresponds ideally to the lost High King of Ireland.

Cosmological Divisions

Originally, of course, there were no demarcated boundaries in Ireland. The earliest tribespeople had no fields to cultivate, no stock to pasture, no goods to store. They took what nature gave wherever it was provided. Yet all people, like all animals, recognize territorial limits, and presumably the ancient tribes and families drew mental boundaries around the stretch of country they regarded as their own. That does not mean that they were confined to that area and knew nothing of the world beyond it. The urge to travel and see new places is not just a modern development. Nomadic people, such as the native Australians, make ritual journeys far beyond their own regions, and their mythological geography extends over a continent. By certain paths, the gods walked through the entire country, creating its landmarks and forms of life. Aboriginal pilgrims take the same paths and repeat their journeys between the sacred creation centers. Large areas of their country are thus made known to them.

In Stone Age Ireland, there were many autonomous tribes, each inhabiting a district with its own, integral mythological cycle. Yet, at the same time, every tribal region had its part in a greater mythological cycle that encompassed the whole island.

In later times, when boundaries were formally established and denoted by landmarks, the primordial state was commemorated once a year, at the November feast of Samhain, or Hallowe'en. Ghosts and archaic spirits were then loosed upon the world and, as the boundaries dissolved between the living and the dead, so for a brief period were all the land boundaries removed throughout Ireland. Chaos claimed its period of supremacy, and bands of mummers made the rounds, representing the anarchic demons that prevailed throughout the world before the institution of order.

In defiance of the psychic threat to the order of the entire realm, the High King of Ireland held a Hallowe'en feast at Tara, attended by the national hierarchy. Alwyn and Brinley Rees, in their book, *Celtic*

Heritage, picture the scene within the royal hall. "On this night of mis-
chief and confusion, the four provincial kings and their people sat four-
square around the king of Ireland, symbolizing and asserting the cosmic
structure of the state and of society while chaos reigned outside."

The maintenance of land divisions as symbols of the ordered
state was an important part of the war against chaos. From the beginning of agriculture, probably in the early part of the fourth millennium BC, fields and settlements were enclosed by physical barriers,
but the larger divisions between clans and tribal territories were preserved only by custom and memory. It was therefore necessary at the
beginning of every summer to reestablish the traditional lines by ceremonies of "beating the bounds." Processions led by priests and chiefs
made a circuit of the district, inspecting the boundary marks and the
ways between them. Along with natural features, such as trees, springs,
boulders, and hilltops, markers were provided by the erect stones and
megalithic monuments that legendary ancestors had placed there for
all eternity. To move or destroy them was a sacrilegious act, hostile to
the entire order of society.

From early times, the whole of Ireland was divided up in various ways to reflect the prevailing mythology. The sons of Partholón
divided it into four and the Nemedians into three parts. Five legendary brothers, the sons of a Fir Bolg ruler, inherited it as five provinces, setting the traditional pattern that continued into historical
times. According to the *Lebor Gabála,* "That is the division of the
provinces of Ireland which shall endure for ever, as the Fir Bolg
divided them."

The five original units were Ulster in the north, Leinster in the
east, Connacht in the west, and two divisions of the southern province, Munster. That implies that there was then no permanent central
authority and that the national assembly was presided over in turn by
the five kings. The eldest of the five brothers, Sláinge the Fir Bolg,
ruler of Leinster, was said to be the first High King of Ireland and
to have died at the end of his year's reign. Two ancient mounds are

claimed as his place of burial, Duma Sláinge at Leighlinbridge on the river Barrow and the Hill of Slane north of Dublin.

Typical of the cosmological pattern of old Ireland was that each social unit, from the province to the single hearth, reproduced the whole. Thus, it is said in the bardic records that the five provinces were each subdivided into five parts. This was done in the sixth century BC when Ugaine Mór was High King. Before his death, he apportioned the country between his twenty-five children. Perhaps in memory of this, early Christian Ireland was divided into twenty-five dioceses.

With the coming of the Sons of Mil, identified as the Gaelic people, Ireland received the classical, cosmological imprint, typical of Bronze Age symbolism. First, the country was divided into two halves and then into four quarters, each half containing six tribes and each quarter three, making twelve tribes in all. A manuscript quoted in Eoin MacNeill's *Celtic Ireland* says:

> The Gaedhil have twelve free or noble races. Six of them are in Conn's half, viz., the race of Conn, the race of Cian, the race of Araide who are the Cruithnig [Picts], the race of Fiatu who are the Ulidians, the race of Riata, the race of Nia Corb who are the Leinstermen. The other six are in Mugh's half: the race of Eoghan, the race of Fiachu, the race of Fiatu, the race of Ceide, the race of Bardine, the race of Cas. These are the free states of Ireland.

The traditional twofold division is marked by a ridge of gravel mounds, the Eiscir Riada, across the shortest central width of Ireland from Galway Bay to Dublin. There is much lore about these two halves, how they came into being, and their contrasting symbolic characters. In cosmological terms, they represented the first stage of creation, the separation of light from darkness and the corresponding polarities of male and female, above and below, the active (yang) and the receptive (yin). The northern half had the overall kingship and the male attributes of industry and inventiveness, while the southern half was the home of music and poetry. A similar polarity, in the Isle of Man, has previously been mentioned, and it seems to occur spontaneously in lands everywhere. The north Britons, Germans, French, and Italians are generally regarded as being more "hard" than the "soft" southerners. Even in the small island of Barbados, the southern people are thought of as more gentle and indolent than the bustling inhabitants of the northern part. The most obvious example, of course, is the religious and political tension in modern Ireland between the industrious northerners and the traditionally more easygoing people of the south.

The second stage in the ritual division of Ireland was into the four provinces—north, south, east, and west—similar to those that exist today. Following the primary separation of the two halves, representing the winter and summer halves of the year, the quartering allowed further symbolism: the four directions, winds, corners of the earth, seasons of the year, and so on. Even at this stage, the divisions supported an elaborate metaphysical system, each quarter acquiring a variety of symbolic attributes.

The Irish word for a province means "a fifth part," so there were not just four provinces but five. The original pentarchy, attributed to the Fir Bolg rulers, consisted of Ulster, Leinster, Connacht, and two halves of Munster, east and west. Their focus and meeting point was the Hill of Uisnech in Westmeath. At some later period, the two parts of Munster were united, and another province, Meath, was formed around the national center. The creation of this "province of kingship" no doubt reflected the growing elaboration of society and the need for a strong, permanent central authority.

The last of the major divisions of Ireland probably took place at the same time that Meath was established, for it completes the cosmological pattern implied by the arrangement of four quarters round a center. This final division was of each quarter into three parts, making twelve sections in all. They correspond to the twelve "free or noble races" of Ireland and to the twelve hours of the day, months of the years, signs of the zodiac, and gods of the classical pantheon.

Traditions of the Center

The central point of Ireland is located within the former national sanctuary, a district within the former central province, Meath, whose Irish name, Midhe, may simply mean "Middle." In it were included the present county of Westmeath, together with parts of Meath, Longford, Monaghan, Cavan, Offaly, and Kildare.

From the beginning of historical times, the ritual state center and seat of the High King was upon the Hill of Tara in the part of Meath formerly called Brega. Five roads led to it from the five provinces, and it acquired the symbols and prestige of the national omphalos. For purposes of administration and assembly, Tara was naturally well placed. Yet it is nowhere near the geographical center of Ireland, which lies more than thirty miles away to the west, in County Westmeath.

This central area, the former sanctuary, is wilder than the fertile lands around Tara, and it is much less accessible. To the east, it is cut off by lakes and bogs, and to the west, by the river Shannon flowing through Lough Ree. The approach from the south is made difficult by bogs and streams, and the Inny River borders it to the north. It lies between the towns of Mullingar and Athlone and measures about twenty miles across. Close together in the center of this district are found the traditional omphalos stone of Ireland, the central mountain, and several places and monuments that are said to mark the country's middle point.

The central mountain is the Hill of Uisnech, situated at the hub of the circle made by Ireland's twelve sacred mountains and the legendary source of twelve sacred rivers. Mythologically, it is like central mountains everywhere, the place of original revelation and the beginning of culture. The earliest kings were installed there, and the first sacred flame in Ireland was lit upon its summit.

The legends of Uisnech and its central position in the island give evidence that it was established as the symbolic focus of the nation long before the rise of Tara. Even when Tara was made the royal capital, traditionally by Ollamh Fódhla in 714, its kings acknowledged the priority of Uisnech as the national omphalos and generation center. They attended the Feast of Beltane there, when the beginning of the year was celebrated together with the beginning of their own race. Fires were put out all over the country and were rekindled from the Druidic bonfire on the Hill of Uisnech.

On the southwest flank of Uisnech, in a sloping, grassy meadow visible from the nearby road, stands a remarkable pillar of rock, Ail na Mirenn, the Stone of Divisions. It is a natural, apparently volcanic formation, about sixteen feet tall, broken up by cracks and fissures. Its base forms a hollow, and around it are the barely perceptible traces of an earthen platform. A deep hole in its summit was drilled early in the twentieth century, when a flagpole was erected on the rock and was made the focus of political, nationalist meetings.

According to the medieval chronicler, Giraldus Cambrensis, the Stone of Divisions "is said to be the navel of Ireland." The same name is given to it in an old Irish poem that hints that, like the Rock of Foundation in Jerusalem, it was also said to be the place where the Flood subsided and to contain the stopper that holds it down. Other legends confirm its ancient character as the central pillar of Ireland, the peg by which the social order was held together, and the pole on which it revolved. It was sacred to Ériu, the Milesian queen-goddess and proprietary spirit of Ireland, whose tomb is located beneath it.

Explaining the name of this stone, an old Irish text, *The Settling of the Manor of Tara,* tells how, early in the Christian era, the nobles wished to establish the limits of the royal domain. An expert geographer or geomancer, Fintan, was summoned to Tara, and from there the whole court proceeded to Uisnech, where Fintan recited the entire history of the country from the days of its first inhabitants. He then confirmed its time-honored system of divisions and boundaries. Five provinces had their meeting point at the Hill of Uisnech, and to mark the exact spot, Fintan erected the Stone of Divisions and inscribed upon it five "ridges." Around it, he defined the sections of land belonging to each province within the sanctuary. To complete

Figure 42. The Stone of Divisions at Uisnech is a remarkable natural outcropping that has acquired many of the legends of a national omphalos. Five of its fissures are said to represent the five provinces that came together at that spot, the central point of Ireland.

his work of reconstituting the traditional order, he described the symbolic attributes of each quarter of Ireland.

It cannot be expected that such an outstanding natural landmark as the Stone of Divisions should happen to stand at the precise central point. The spot determined by geography is about six miles to the west of it, and from that spot the Celtic geomancers fixed the boundaries of Ireland's provinces. Its exact location has long been forgotten, but its legend haunts the entire district. Everyone there seems to know about the center of Ireland, but there is wide disagreement about where it actually is. About a dozen different sites each have their local supporters, emphasizing the need that every nation seems to experience, of identifying its own midpoint and navel.

Figures 43–46. The reputed
centers of Ireland, all in
the same district, include
Coolatore Hill (opposite
above), the Pinnacle at
Kilkenny West (opposite
below), the Hill of Berries
(above), and a cross at the
southern end of Lough Ree.

The range of legendary centers of Ireland stretches for about eighteen miles, from the Hill of Uisnech in the east to the far side of Lough Ree. Included with Uisnech and the Stone of Divisions are the following:

Killare. In *Annals of Westmeath, Ancient and Modern,* published in 1907 by James Woods, a native of Mullingar who rose by way of journalism to become the local historian, the center of Ireland is said to be at Killare. This is a small, decayed village, consisting now of little more than an inn at a crossroads, below the western slope of the Hill of Uisnech. Formerly, it was a place of religious importance with an abbey and three churches. The historian Camden believed it to be the town of Laberos mentioned in Ptolemy's *Geographica.* It is associated with St. Brigit, Ireland's most popular female saint, who took her religious vows on the Hill of Uisnech. In the village are the ruins of her old church and St. Brigit's holy well, still frequented and once a famous place of pilgrimage. Killare's Uisnech Inn shows on its signboard the nearby Stone of Divisions, depicted with its traditional five ridges. Preserved there by its present proprietor, Mrs. Mulligan, is a manuscript history of ancient Uisnech by a local scholar, John Stokes.

Knockcosgrey Hill. In Ian Robertson's *Blue Guide: Ireland,* it is said that this hill above the ruins of Killeenbrack Castle, about a mile south of Killare, is considered to be the geographical center of Ireland.

Coolatore Hill. North of Moate and two and one-half miles southwest of Knockcosgrey Hill, a stone on this prominent hilltop is locally claimed as the center.

Moydrum Hill. Further to the west, about three miles east of Athlone, this hill is included in the list of Irish centers compiled by Gearoid O'Brien, the Athlone scholar and librarian. Its legend may be modern, judging from the central television mast on its summit.

The Pinnacle, Kilkenny West. The "center of Ireland" legend seem to have attached itself to every notable hill and monument in the district. Six miles northeast of Athlone, between Glasson and Kilkenny West, is a ruined stone tower, about twenty feet tall, standing upon a hill. It was put up in 1769 by a landowner, Nataniel Lowe, whose main residence was at Lowville, County Galway, twenty-five miles away to the west on the far side of Lough Ree. There, he built a similar tower, and the story is that from it he communicated by flag with his agent at Kilkenny West. The Pinnacle, as it is called locally, has attracted several different legends. Among other things, it is said to be the entrance to an underground tunnel and an ancient round tower. Most firmly established is the belief that it is the central pillar of Ireland. This was recorded over a hundred years ago, and it is still affirmed today, both locally and in several guidebooks.

The cross opposite Carberry Island. On a hill on the south shore of Lough Ree, two miles north of Athlone, a large stone cross was erected in Holy Year, 1962, by the Lough Ree Yacht Club, the implication being that it marked the center of Ireland.

The Hill of Berries. Two miles north of Athlone, near the southwest end of Lough Ree, a fine clump of beech trees on a hill makes a prominent landmark. A landowner is said to have planted it many years ago as a memorial to his daughter, who died young, and the legend that it also marks the center of the country is locally well known. Gearoid O'Brien remembers an old ticket inspector at Dublin Station who would point passengers to the Athlone train with the words, "For the Hill of Berries and the Heart of Ireland!"

Hodson's Pillar. Two miles north from the Hill of Berries, on the western shore of Lough Ree, the Hodson's Bay Hotel faces a small islet bearing a ruined tower. Nothing seems to be known about the history of this monument, but the inevitable claim is that it was put there to mark the center of Ireland. This is

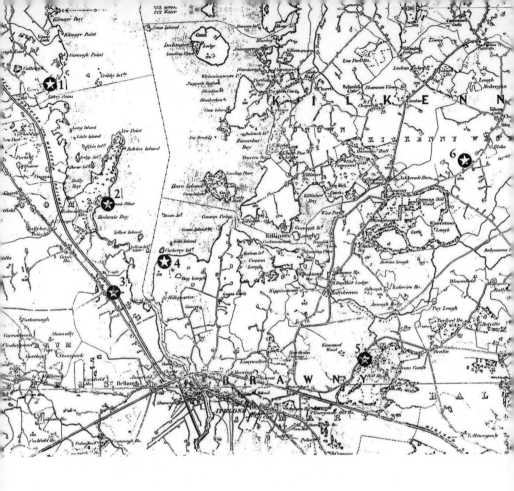

Figure 47. Claimed as the center of Ireland are many sites in a small area near Athlone and the southern end of Lough Ree:

1) The geographical center of gravity, located by the Ordnance Survey
2) The pillar in Hodson's Bay
3) The Hill of Berries
4) A modern cross
5) Moydrum Hill
6) The Pinnacle, Kilkenny West
7) The ancient centerpoint for the ritual divisions of Ireland
8) Coolatore Hill
9) Knockcosgrey Hill
10) Killare
11) The Hill of Uisnech
12) The Stone of Divisions

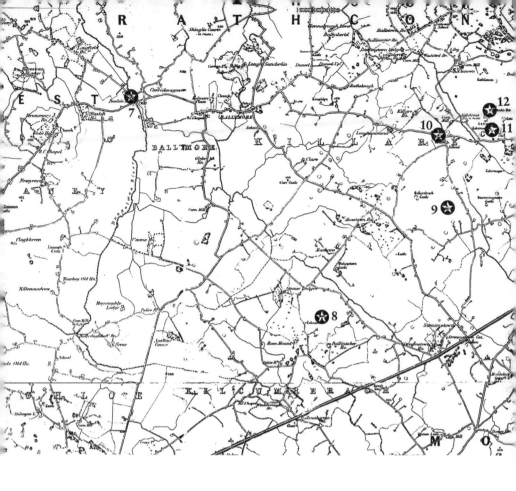

stated on a metal plaque on the shore in front of the hotel. The plaque was ceremonially unveiled about ten years ago by the governor of the State of Georgia, who happen to be nearby on holiday at the time.

Carnagh Bay. Ignoring all legends, the Irish Ordnance Survey has fixed the geographical center of the country "in the Townland of Carnagh East, Co. Roscommon, on the west shore of Lough Ree, opposite the Cribby Islands and 5½ miles NNW of Athlone Town, where the 8° meridian West meets the 53° 30' North latitude."

There is also a popular belief that the center of Ireland is halfway between Dublin and Galway. That means that it lies to the east of Athlone, which boasts of being Ireland's central town. For this reason, it has several times been proposed that Athlone would be the ideal capital for all Ireland. This idea goes back to at least the thirteenth century. Standing on the boundary between Leinster and Connacht, where the bridge, replacing the ancient ford, crosses the Shannon, Athlone is Ireland's natural centre of communications.

All these reputed centers of Ireland are clustered in one small district, and the true center, as calculated in this chapter, lies amid them. It is located about a mile west of Ballymore, on the northwest side of the bridge over the Tang River, where a cluster of ancient stones marks the site of a ruined mound. This is Ireland's secret heartland, green and rural, scenically undramatic, little visited, yet full of secluded shrines and antiquities that, together with its unique legends, reveal the special significance of the area as the national sanctuary, appointed by nature and hallowed by centuries of ancient priestcraft. "According to the usage of the Gaels," wrote Geoffrey Keating in his seventeenth-century *History of Ireland,* "it was the mensal land of the Irish sovereigns, and exempt from the laws, governments and taxation of every prince in Ireland, except the Sovereign Prince (Ard-Rígh) himself."

The Domain of the High King

The 600-foot Hill of Uisnech is not spectacular, merely a large swelling, like an English down, broad topped and with no obvious summit. A megalithic ruin, St. Patrick's Bed, stands on a high point, and nearby is St. Patrick's Well, but there is little apparent evidence of its prehistoric royal assemblies at the Mayday Feast of Bel. Everything is below the surface, and when the hilltop was excavated in the 1930s, archaeologists found impressive remains, including ashes and burned earth from great bonfires, a sanctuary approached by a ceremonial road, and the footings of a large building that Professor Macalister identified as the hall of Tuathal Teuchtmar, high king in the second century AD.

The most significant aspect of Uisnech is the view from the top of it, to every quarter of Ireland and most of the thirty-two counties. Michael Dames has recently written about this, showing how bonfires on the surrounding ring of hilltops would have communicated their light to an outer circle and thence to every coast and corner of the country. Many of these high places mark sunrise or some other astronomical event on the festival days at Uisnech and have legendary connections with the old center, hinting at the ceaseless round of myth, music, and ritual by which the Druids maintained a religious spell over the entire island.

Closely surrounding the Hill of Uisnech are a great number of ancient castles, mostly now vanished or in ruins. The fiercest resistance to Norman and English invaders took place around the central sanctuary, and it was one of the last districts to be fully pacified under foreign rule.

Legends of Uisnech as the national center begin at the time of the Nemedian invasion, when Midhe, their arch-Druid, kindled upon it the first sacred fire in all Ireland. This set the precedent that St. Patrick followed when, in the fifth century, he symbolized the implanting of Christianity by his Easter bonfire on the Hill of Slane. Midhe's fire had a similar effect on the religious authorities of his time. They met in conclave to denounce it, but Midhe stifled their protest by cutting out their tongues, making a heap of them, and sitting enthroned upon them on the Hill of Uisnech.

The name of the central province, Meath or Midhe, has several traditional derivations: from Arch-Druid Midhe; from the epithet, *midhe* (evil), which the priests applied to his intrusive bonfire; or from a much later event, when Tuathal Teuchtmar took a neck (*meicibe*) of land from each of the other provinces to form the high king's domain. This implies that the central sanctuary around Uisnech was regarded as the common "head" to the four quarters of Ireland. With the addition of the "necks," a fifth, royal province completed the national hierarchy.

Upon the Hill of Uisnech, King Tuathal planted an ash tree, a conventional symbol of the world-pole, as the focus of seasonal ceremonies, culminating in the grand assembly at Beltane. This was attended by all the chief men of Ireland—the kings, priests, and judges from each of the provinces. State councils and law courts enacted the authority of the High King and affirmed the ritual order of his realm. After the solemnities came the popular festival, with the customary games and competitions. A traditional account is given in Woods's *Annals of Westmeath, Ancient and Modern.*

> Music, history, poetry, genealogy, formed special features of the entertainment. The two great fires were lighted in honour of Beal, the sun god, between which the cattle were driven in order to preserve them from sickness during the coming year. There were also great feats of arms and horsemanship performed, and prizes were distributed by the Ard Rígh on each day of the feast. Then followed the great fair of Uisneach, the special features of which were three principal markets—one for livestock and horses, one for clothes and food and a third was railed off for the use of foreign merchants who sold gold and silver articles and fine raiment. At the great banquet of Uisneach it was the privilege of the King of Oriel to sit next the King of Ireland, but he sat at such a distance that his sword just reached the head of the Ard Rígh, and to him also belonged the honour of presenting every third drinking horn to the king.

Further described is the delicate manner in which the provincial kings paid tribute to their sovereign. "Each of these petty kings was bound to wear on one of his fingers a hero's ring of red gold, which, on the breaking up of the convention, he left on the seat he occupied." Moreover, "every lord of a manor or chieftain who attended presented a horse and arms to the King of Connaught on account of the very considerable portion of land that was taken off his territory to form the mensal lands of the high king."

There is no apparent difference between this Celtic national assembly, held in the central district of the country, and the similarly located Scandinavian Al-thing. The Celtic examples, Irish and Manx, are certainly older, but all these central, ritualized festivals arose from the same type of society, symbolically structured under a national religious authority and based on the same cosmological pattern.

Throughout this inquiry, we have been looking for the most likely period when these societies were first instituted, and the evidence points ever more clearly to the Bronze Age, beginning in the third millennium BC. Relics of that period, including some of the finest gold and jeweled objects that have ever been crafted, imply an equally magnificent social order, solarly orientated, enriched by an heroic mythology, and guided in all its processes by a cycle of ceremony that varied but never ended throughout the years and ages.

The legend of Uisnech, which offers the greatest claim for its antiquity, makes it the original site of the Stonehenge temple. The story is given in *The History of the Kings of England by Geoffrey of Monmouth,* from the twelfth century. A British king of ancient days, Aurelius Ambrosius, required a noble monument to commemorate victims of a treacherous massacre by the Saxons, whom he had just defeated. His wise counselor, Merlin, said that the finest architectural work in the British Isles was the Giant's Round at Mount Killaraus in Ireland, and that he should procure it.

The king's brother, Uther Pendragon, invaded Ireland with an army of fifteen thousand, defeated the Irish, and proceeded to Mount Killaraus. This was the Hill of Uisnech under the name of the village at its foot, Killare. The Giant's Round was a ring of enormous stones, put together so skillfully that no one could move them. After the soldiers had tried unsuccessfully to do so, Merlin used his art to dismantle the stones, transport them to England, and erect them again on Salisbury Plain.

There is a strange coincidence between this story and another legend of Uisnech that provides a further link with Stonehenge. Merlin said that the stones had been brought to Uisnech from Africa by giants, who used them as "washing stones"—pouring water over them to provide healing baths. The washing stones of Uisnech are heard of again, in a quite different period and context, when St. Patrick cursed them and thus deprived them of their virtues. The reputedly medicinal virtues of the stones at Stonehenge are mentioned by several early writers. Many of them, the foreign bluestones, were brought to Stonehenge from a distant region some time before 2000 BC. Their original quarry is thought to be in southwest Wales. It is not known when or how they were first taken from Wales, so it is quite possible that the old histories are correct and the stones of Stonehenge once stood within the sacred precinct at Uisnech. If so, they would surely have been positioned at the ancient geographical center of Ireland, identified in the following pages.

The Geographical Center and the Divisions of the Provinces

In the previous book, *Twelve-Tribe Nations,* the central point of Ireland was discovered and was shown to have been the focus of a regular geometric pattern that divided the country first into four quarters, defining the boundary limits of the four provinces, and secondly into twelve sections, three to each quarter. As well as these and other boundary points, the pattern included the extreme southern, eastern, western, and northwestern apexes of the island and marked its main axis.

To confirm the accuracy of this system, Christine Rhone carefully constructed it on an overlay that, when applied to a large-scale map of Ireland, exactly fitted these main features of its physical and political geography. With the benefit of the evidence that has since come to light in the Isle of Man, Shetland, and elsewhere, this subject is again approached, with greater confidence and certainty, for the principles behind the ancient location of Ireland's center are the same as those discovered in other countries.

The first thing to look for is Ireland's main axis. This is the longest line that can be drawn through the country, dividing it into two more or less equal halves. From what has previously been learned, it appears that this line should begin at the southernmost point of the country, creating the image of a world-tree growing upward from its roots. The southernmost point of Ireland is Cape Clear in County Cork. The direct line from there to the northernmost point, Mali Head, does not make an equal division of the island, nor is it the longest line that can be drawn across it. From Cape Clear, the longest line that can be drawn through Ireland goes to the northeast corner, Torr Head in County Antrim, 298 miles away. That line also divides the country into two halves and so provides its main axis.

This represents the polar axis, north to south. The cross axis is the line between the eastern and western extremities. In Ireland, they are clearly defined. The easternmost point is Burr Point in County Down, with the sacred islet, Burial Island, beyond it, and the westernmost is the farthest of the once-inhabited Blaskett Islands, which is also the most western point of Europe.

The point where these two lines intersect is the center of Ireland.

Another means of finding the center is to join diagonally the four coastal termini of the boundaries of Ulster and Munster. This produces a cross, at the center of which is the same, previously established, central point. The implication is that from that spot the ancient surveyors of Ireland determined by geometric reckoning the original borders between the provinces.

The present provincial boundaries are not quite as they originally were. What is loosely called Ulster today is the six counties—Londonderry, Antrim, Fermanagh, Tyrone, Armagh, and Down—that constitute the British territory of Northern Ireland. Properly speaking, Ulster contains three other counties—Monaghan, Cavan, and

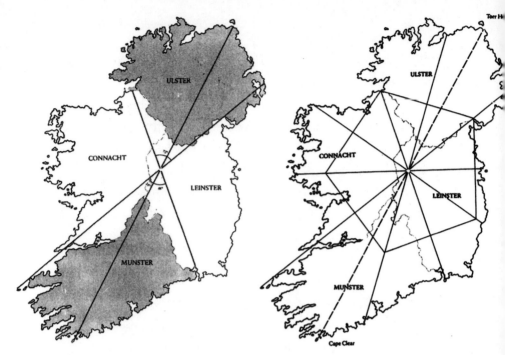

Figure 48a (left). The ritual division of Ireland into provinces was carried out from a central point, which is discovered by reconstructing the original scheme. First, the main axis from the most southern point of the country, Cape Clear, is extended to the most distant point on the opposite coast, Torr Head in Ulster. Another axis is drawn between Ireland's eastern and western extremities, and the central point is where the two lines cross. This is confirmed when the coastal boundary points, east and west, of Ulster and Munster are joined diagonally and their crossing is found to be at the same spot. One of these diagonals, when extended, joins the extreme eastern and western points of Ireland.

Figure 48b (right). Where these lines meet at the center, they form angles of 24°, 48°, and 72°, indicating a regular geometric division. The most obvious figure is a pentagon, with one of its sides defined by the line joining the extremities of Ulster's border. This develops naturally into a ten-part division, which may represent an early stage in the geomantic arrangement of Ireland. The final, twelve-part figure that was adapted from it is shown in figure 49. In the ten-part scheme, the original axis (broken line) is not included in the symmetry.

Donegal. At one time, between the reigns of King John and Queen Elizabeth I, it also contained Louth, but that county is now correctly in Leinster, and the eastern terminus of the boundary between Ulster and Leinster is at the head of Carlingford Lough above Warrenpoint, where three counties meet.

The western extremity of Ulster's border with Connacht is at the mouth of the small river issuing from Lough Melvin to the west of Bundoran.

In the south, Munster's border with Leinster ends at Waterford Harbor, at the confluence of the rivers Barrow and Suir, where three counties meet—Waterford, Wexford, and Kilkenny.

The original border between Munster and Connacht is down the estuary of the river Shannon, which separates the counties of Clare on the north bank from Kerry to the south. In Charles II's reign, Clare was included in Munster, but geographically and traditionally it is part of Connacht.

From the outline maps (figure 48a and b), it can be seen that the line from the eastern end of the Ulster–Leinster border, across the island and down the old dividing line between Munster and Connacht, is, when projected, the same line as that between Ireland's eastern and western extremities.

A remarkable feature of the diagram, as so far developed, is that the lines from the central point to the two extremities of Ulster's border, east and west, are precisely equal, both seventy-two miles long. Moreover, the angle at which they meet is of 72°. This is the fifth part division of a 360° circle, and it implies a regular five-sided figure, a pentagon, dividing the country into five or ten sections around the center. The boundary between East Munster and West Munster ends at the head of Cork Harbor, and the line from the center to that point accords with the pentagonal symmetry.

The likelihood is that this diagram (figure 48b) represents an early stage in the ritual dividing of Ireland, when five provinces met at the central point that was not at that time enclosed within a central province.

The creation of Meath, from lands contributed by each of the old provinces, was doubtless made necessary by the emergence of a supreme national authority, the High King. Within royal Meath, the other four provinces (East and West Munster now being united) had their own sections and enjoyed certain rights, but the High King was paramount, thus increasing his prestige and his influence over the provincial rulers.

In the old myths, gods, kings, and heroes are never clearly distinguished from each other, and the legendary rulers of old Ireland are referred to as divinities. They were indeed sacred kings of the type known throughout the ancient world, representatives of the solar deity and invested with godlike powers. Their duties were largely ritualistic, to maintain the religious calendar and festivals and to enact throughout their lives the ideal, orderly constitution of the realm.

As shown by many examples in *Twelve-Tribe Nations,* the kingdoms of such rulers were characteristically divided into four provinces, each with three tribal divisions, imitating the pattern of seasons and months. The king of each province took precedence over two lesser rulers, and in that order, seated in their respective quarters around the High King enthroned at the center, the twelve kings reproduced the cosmological pattern on which the realm was founded.

In imitation of his model, the sun, the High King made a regular circuit of his kingdom, holding court at the chief provincial sanctuaries. This is described in the eleventh-century *Book of Rights.* A poem tells of the king of Cashel, in his capacity of High King, traveling sunwise around the island and being received by a succession of kings, each of whom escorted him on the next stage of his journey. This was the usual procedure under a sacred kingship. King Solomon in the great days of Israel did the same thing, as described in 1 Kings 4, appointing twelve tribal rulers whose duties included entertaining the king and his court for one month of the year. The implication is that he made a yearly judicial and festal round of his kingdom, following the sun in its progress through the twelve houses of the zodiac.

The legendary twelve noble races of Ireland were possibly the clans or septs from which the twelve kings were elected. This pattern of twelve kings, warriors, or followers with a central thirteenth as leader is constantly repeated in traditional Irish lore. In the royal hall of Ulster, King Conchobar held court in the same style as the High King, taking his place at the center while his twelve chief warriors reclined on couches around him. A similar pattern is implied by the legendary twelve kings of Munster, the twelve kings of Galway, and many other such groups.

The old order was maintained by the early Celtic Church. Throughout the Celtic world, and farther afield, foundation legends tell of twelve missionaries with a leader who began the conversion of the country. Later, these twelve anchorites, who probably represented the twelve notes of their perpetually sustained sacred chant, were replaced by twelve great monastic colleges with twelve holy men as their chiefs. Early in the sixth century, St. Finnian reaffirmed the traditional model, establishing his central monastery at Clonard in Meath and ruling the church through a council of the so-called Twelve Apostles of Ireland, each from one of the twelve provincial monasteries. This reflected the previous religious organization of the country, when St. Finnian's predecessor, the metropolitan arch-Druid, sat above a council of twelve chief Druids from the twelve divisions of Ireland.

Sacred kingship implies a ruler who represents the solar deity— Apollo, Odin, Arthur—and is served by twelve lesser god-kings, corresponding to the twelve zodiacal signs that structure and govern the cosmos. Under their rule, the country is divided by radial lines from its center into twelve sections, each with its own astrological attributes and each associated with an episode in the twelve-part national myth and a note in the twelve-tone scale of sacred music.

With the institution of sacred kingship in Ireland, the former, archaic division of the country into five provinces and ten sections, all with a common center, was adapted to create a twelve-part division within a new ordering of the provinces, four at the four quarters of the realm and one in the middle.

The method by which the original pentagon was adapted to accommodate twelve sections, without altering the positions of the

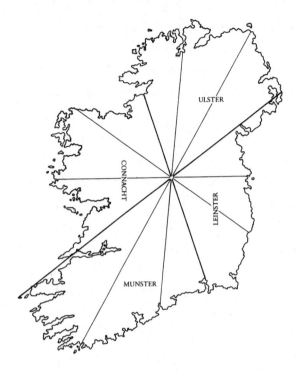

Figure 49. In the twelve-part division of Ireland, adapted from the previous ten divisions, the main axis from Cape Clear to Torr Head is symmetrically included. Each of the four provinces around Meath has three sections. The pattern corresponds to the legendary twelve free races of old Ireland.

four provincial boundary marks, is shown in figure 49. Because the shape of Ireland is longer than it is wide, the regular ten-part division of the country gives three sections to both the eastern and the western provinces, while the northern and southern provinces have two each. Yet each quarter should have three sections. This means that the angle of 72°, formed by the axes between the border limits of Ulster and Munster, is divided into three angles of 24°, thus producing three narrower but longer sections in those two provinces.

This operation allowed Ireland's main axis to feature in the scheme. The main axis is the line from the southernmost point to Torr Head, the point of Ireland nearest to Scotland. Together with the line between the eastern and western extremities, it forms an angle of 24°, and this defines one of the three narrower sections in both Ulster and Munster. The inclusion of this axis, the symbolic pole of Ireland, is in keeping with the twelvefold pattern of cosmology and the divine authority attached to sacred kingship.

The transition from five provinces around a pivot to the solar pattern of four triply-divided quarters around Meath appears to mark the rise of a solar-oriented sacred king. The question once again is, when did this take place? Tradition makes it the work of King Tuathal early in the second century. He, it is said, first created the royal, central province of Meath. That same period, at the beginning of the Christian era, is thought by historians to have been the heyday of Irish sacred kingship. According to that view, it is wrong to look for the origin of the ritually divided, twelve-part realm in the splendor of the Bronze Age. Could such an elaborate state system have survived from such a distant period? The bardic histories of old Ireland paint a picture of successive upheavals, revolutions, and invasions, the disappearance of old dynasties and races, and the triumphs of new cults and cultures. Yet behind these dramatic changes was an element of tradition and continuity. Despite all the political regroupings of units, the principal borders within the country were likely to remain constant, and the strong sense of tradition in prehistoric societies would always have encouraged a revival of the original ritual pattern. It is still possible, therefore, to locate the origin of Ireland's twelve-fold divisions where anthropological evidence seems to indicate, in the same period as the building of Stonehenge in about 2000 BC.

Another point in favor of ancient origins, raised in a previous chapter, is the connection between land surveying and astronomy. The priests of Neolithic societies observed the heavens and orientated their primitive temples in accordance with the seasonal positions of the heavenly bodies. Stonehenge, the first known and most perfect Bronze Age temple, has been found by Gerald Hawkins and other astronomers to feature twelve principal lines of sight toward the twelve extreme positions of the sun and moon. This implies recognition of the traditional twelve gods and a corresponding division of land and people into the customary twelve-tribe order. Examples of this twelve-part system of dividing the heavens—which then requires a similar twelve-part division of the sanctified country that reflects the heavenly order—occur in Babylon, Egypt, China, and widely throughout the ancient world. It is no anachronism, therefore, to attribute an equal antiquity to the ritual division of Ireland.

The Once and Future High King:
A Helpful Suggestion

It is obviously impossible today to restore the traditional sacred constitution of old Ireland, even if anyone wanted to do so. Yet there are certain advantages in the old federal constitution that might helpfully be considered again, especially where two peoples of different origins and forms of religion occupy a single island and therefore have many interests in common.

In ancient Ireland, there were many different tribes, deriving according to their legends from Scythia, Iberia, and other distant lands, and including Picts, Scots, and Brigantians, whose main territory was in the north of England. We hear of battles and rivalries between them, but their differences overall were transcended by their common allegiance—when it suited them, at least—to a higher authority, the king of all Ireland.

When the thirty-two southern counties of Ireland gained independence from Great Britain, much thought was given to installing a constitutional monarch as head of state. The crown of Ireland was indeed offered to the chiefs of the three main dynastic families, but each of them refused it in favor of an elected Taoiseach.

The weakness in this proposal was that it did not go far enough, nor could it have done in the circumstances of the time. Today, however, things are different and far more urgent. The anomalous situation, that six counties of Ulster (omitting three others that properly belong to that province) adhere to the British crown, has become more and more aggravating. Relations between northern and southern Ireland, and between Northern Ireland and Britain, are endemically uneasy.

The only lasting remedy for this state of affairs is on the idealistic level, transcending the level of self-interest and grievances. Rather than tinkering around with well-meaning compromises, which irritate far more people than are gratified by them, it seems necessary to review the situation as a whole and to perceive the ideal resolution that accords with the noble tradition of ancient Ireland.

The installation of a High King over all Ireland would affirm the geographical reality while allowing each part of the nation to be as independent as it chooses within its own borders. This could be achieved by, for example, returning self-government to each of the four provinces—Ulster being at first limited to the six counties each with an elected governor and an internal constitution of its own choosing. The four governors would elect or nominate in turn the High King of Ireland. His duties would be purely ceremonial and cultural, but initiatives agreed upon by all four provinces would be founded or carried out by his authority.

One can imagine the High King as a dignified, scholarly figure, with an honorable reputation and no political ambitions. His capital is fixed in the central town of Ireland, Athlone. There, under his patronage, are the national institutions of learning and culture and whatever departments of the administration have been entrusted to him by all the four provinces. Each of the provinces has its particular district within the capital, and every royal institution is staffed equally by their representatives.

It is naturally in the interest of all the provinces that the spirit of Ireland herself is honored and satisfied. Thus, a department under the High King is concerned with the well-being of the island as a whole, to ensure that salmon can navigate pure rivers, that ancient monuments are protected. The national museum and a university where the Irish and English languages are equally respected are obvious candidates for royal patronage. Other departments that seem uncontroversially suitable for centralized authority include civil aviation, the postal system, and defense. The learned and gracious king of Ireland is a diplomatic asset, for he is better qualified to receive foreign dignitaries and heads of state than any political leader.

This suggestion is made simply in principle and in outline, without presuming to enter into the details of other people's affairs. It is capable of all kinds of developments and variations within the federal framework. The strength of it is that it merely restores the old, tried-and-true model, involves no innovations, and allows each division of the country to preserve whichever of its laws, customs, and institutions it pleases, while partaking in the administration of whatever they all choose to do in common. It is pitched at a level that engages idealism rather than mere considerations of sectarian advantage. An imaginative, ideally conceived solution to Ireland's dichotomy is more practical and more likely to prove generally acceptable than any amount of petty calculation.

7

THE COSMOLOGICAL
PROTOTYPE

There have been many references in this book to a cosmological code, model, or pattern as the prototype for all the examples of astrologically ordered societies and landscapes that have here been examined. This model has been reviewed fully in a number of previous books, so it needs no further elaboration but is described merely in outline. It is clearly the same as that Egyptian canon of harmonies, referred to by Plato in *Laws* (656–57), which preserved the order of society unchanged "over literally thousands of years"; it has been shown to be the model for Plato's ideal city and also, five hundred years later, for the ideal city of St. John in Revelation, the Heavenly Jerusalem come to earth.

This same model determined the ground plan and symbolism of Stonehenge, the social order of which it was the focus, and, so it now appears, the ritual divisions of Ireland. The occurrence at different times throughout the world of similarly organized twelve-tribe societies, focused upon a rock, a sanctuary, and a sacred king, can only be due to the influence of a common prototype, which must be that traditional code of number and proportion that constitutes the best possible, most rational, and most inclusive image of essential reality.

In its geometric form, the model cosmology is based on the most economical synthesis of the base numbers, 1 to 12, expressed in the simplest way possible, by means of a circle, symbol of the all-inclusive universe. As shown in figure 50, the radius of this circle is 5040, or the numbers 1, 2, 3, 4, 5, 6, and 7, multiplied together, while the quadrant of the circumference is 7920, the product of $8 \times 9 \times 10 \times 11$. The area of each semicircle is the product of the numbers 1 to 11, and the developed scheme is now shown to be held within the framework of the number 12.

Upon the circle is laid, by a certain geometrical process, a square with the same measure round its four sides as the circle's circumference. The perimeter of the circle with radius 5040 is 31,680 (taking pi as 22/7), so the side of the square measures a quarter part of that number, 7920. If a circle is drawn within that square, its diameter is, of course, the same as the square's side, 7920.

The square is the geometric symbol of matter, human logic, and man-made artifacts, as opposed to the heavenly, unending circle. Within the square, the circle represents the ideal earth, with its diameter, 7920, referring to the 7920 miles in the earth's mean diameter. Thus, the diagram so far is of the sanctified earth under the influence of the heavens.

Figure 50 (opposite). The Cosmological Prototype

a) The basic cosmological circle, combining 5040 (the product of the numbers 1–7) with 7920 (the product of 8–11).

b) The square, symbol of matter, with the same perimeter as the circle, is added to the diagram, and the circle it contains is the circle of the Earth, with a diameter of 7920 miles.

c) The space between the circles of the Earth and the cosmos determines the radius, 1080, of the small circles at the four quarters. The radius of the moon is 1080 miles.

d) The diagram is completed with twelve lunar circles, each of radius 1080 (also representing the twelve months, each of 2×1080 years, in the astrological "great year"). This is the basic diagram of the ideal city, nation, or paradisal earth. As a symbol of completeness, it contains all systems of proportion, including the number 7, the symbol of spirit. Here a twenty-eight-pointed figure ($7 \times 4 = 28$) precisely fits all points within the twelve-part framework and corresponds to the twenty-eight constellations within the zodiac.

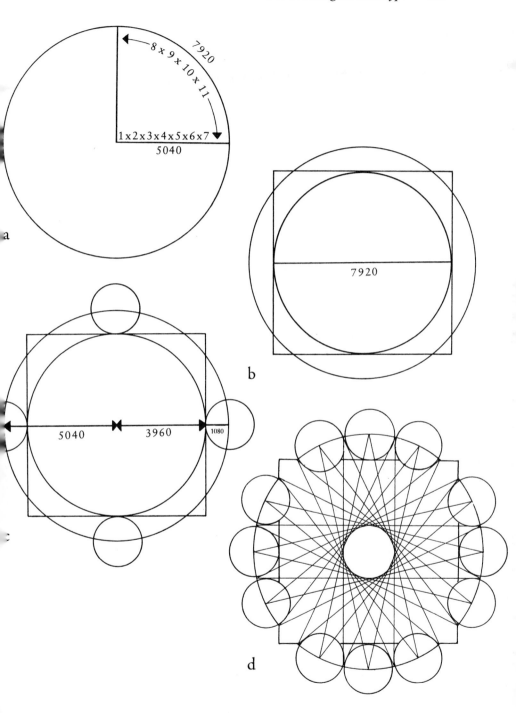

a

b

c

d

The difference between the radii of the two circles, outer and inner, is 5040 − 3960 = 1080. This number, 1080, refers to the 1080 miles in the moon's radius. The moon's true diameter is 2160. In figure 50d, twelve "moons" are added to the diagram, their positions being determined by the meeting points of the original circle and square. Each of their diameters is 2160, so as well as the 2160-mile diameter of the moon, they also represent the 2160 years, the traditional period in which the sun completes its passage through one sign of the zodiac. Twelve such "world months" amount to 25,920 years, in which time the stars revert to their original order and an entire age is accomplished. The diagram is thus, at the same time, a geometric key to "squaring the circle," a scale model of the Earth and moon with their correct dimensions, and an astrological chart or calendar. It also provided the ground plan for state temples and a model for ideal constitutions.

The pole of the universe is inevitably denoted every time one takes a compass to draw a circle. It is represented by the pivot of the compass, revolving but always on the same spot, and by the pit or hole it makes at the center. Completing the basic scheme, another "lunar" circle, with a diameter of 2160, is drawn around the pole.

This diagram perfectly illustrates Plato's astrological city of his *Laws*. The dot in the center is the symbolic pole within the citadel. The inner circle represents the city, and the circle around it is the inhabited earth or, on the scale of Plato's city-state, the extent of land that the community needs to cultivate. Around all, centered on the heavenly circle of circumference 31,680, are the "hills with temples" that surround Plato's community.

The virtue of this cosmological diagram is that it combines every order of number and geometry within its duodecimal framework and expresses in its proportions the "lawful" harmonies of music. Symbolically, it is the all-inclusive image of creation. In it are the months of the year and of the great year, the twelve gods of the zodiac, the twelve types of personality, and the twelve races of mankind, placed around and sharing, each in their own section, the sanctified earth. Properly interpreted, it depicts the correct relationship between the rulers and the people, the intellect and the appetites, humanity and divinity. It is the model from which temples were constructed, sanctuaries and kingdoms were planned, political constitutions were framed. When brought to life by minds that understand its meaning, it is the formula for the nearest possible simulacrum of paradise or the fully perfected individual.

The most important feature of this diagram, and of the cosmology it illustrates, is its center. The dot made by the compass point is the only element in a circle that maintains its position. It is the essence of the whole and symbol of the fixed, eternal laws of nature. This is a God-centered cosmology, subordinating the transient to the unchanging, illusion to reality, matter to spirit, and the gross element in oneself to its natural ruler, the God-centered mind. It is the universal pole, the ideal image of justice.

Examples of national constitutions modeled on this traditional canon, code, or formula range in time from the start of the second millennium BC to the end of the nineteenth century, when the sacred, twelve-tribe order of Madagascar was destroyed by French colonialism. The sanctuary of its central Hova tribe, and its present capital, Antananarivo, is equidistant, 500 miles, from each end of the island. It was essentially the same constitution as those of the Ashanti and other African nations, of the ancient East, of Greek and Celtic realms, and of Nordic countries such as Iceland, which adopted the classical, twelve-fold foundation plan soon after its settlement, in the tenth century.

In the mythologies of all these societies, from India to Scandinavia, the same symbolic numbers recur. One number, for example 1080, is the radius of the moon in miles and of the small circles in the canonical diagram; it appears in the 108 beads of the Hindu or Buddhist rosary, the 10,800 stanzas in the *Rig Veda,* the 10,800 bricks in the Indian fire altar, the 1080 minims in the Jewish hour, the 108,000 years in a season of the Hindu Kali Yuga, the 10,800 years given by Heraclitus as the period between successive destructions of civilizations, and the 1080 pillars of Valhalla, where the shades of 432,000 (equal to 4 × 108,000) Scandinavian heroes feasted in the days of Odin.

In the esoteric science behind all religions, this number, 1080, symbolizes the lunar, subterranean, subconscious, inspirational "night" side of nature. Gnostic theologians of early Christianity, using the priestly science of *gematria,* equated it with the Holy Spirit, for the numerical values of the Greek letters in that phrase add up to 1080. By the same system, 1080 is the symbolic number of such terms as the Fountain of Wisdom, the Earth Spirit and Tartaros, the nether regions. It is the characteristic "yin" number.

On the opposite pole to 1080 is the "yang" solar number 666, symbol of authority and material splendor. The sum of these two opposites is the "number of fusion," 1746, referred to esoterically in the New Testament (Matthew 13:31, for instance) as the "grain of mustard seed" that grew into the world-tree. Another of the key numbers in this same "canonical" group is 3168, from which the founders of Christianity derived the Greek name for Lord Jesus Christ. All these and other principal symbolic numbers feature in the traditional cosmological diagram, where 31,680 measures the perimeters of both the original circle and the square that goes with it.

The most important of such numbers is separately described in *The Dimensions of Paradise,* where the cosmological system to which they belong is set out in detail. Here it is examined only briefly, but some knowledge of it is essential in studying any aspect of ancient or traditionally constituted civilizations, for these were universally based on the same numerical canon. Scholars have always been puzzled by the mysterious yet precise patterns of number that structured mythologies and, at the same time, provided systems of weights and measures, time keeping, astronomical reckoning, and state ritual. These have rarely been studied other than locally, but by comparison

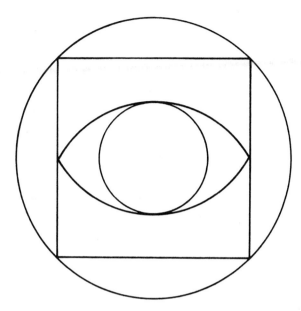

Figure 51. The cosmological circle, with a radius of 5040, is contained within a vesica whose calculated length (twice 5040 multiplied by the square root of 3) is 17,460, a reference to the "number of fusion" (1746) that unites by addition the two symbolic numbers representing the positive, solar (666) and the negative, lunar (1080) principles in nature. The area of the outer circle is therefore 479,001,600, or the numbers 1 to 12 multiplied together.

This image of completeness, formed by the union of the first twelve numbers, is one of the many symbols of the cosmic order that develops from the basic cosmological circle. Upon the universal code of number and proportion, expressed by these figures, the social order of many civilizations has been constructed.

of examples recorded in many different times and parts of the world, it is discovered that all such systems are basically identical and clearly derive from a common origin. The source of all was the numerically codified expression of a perfectly balanced cosmos, the sacred canon of proportions.

To complete this outline of the diagram, the original circle with a radius of 5040 is enclosed within a *vesica,* the first figure of symbolic geometry (figure 51). The longer axis of the vesica is calculated to be 1746, the previously mentioned number of fusion, and that number is also the side of the square containing it. A circle is constructed to contain the square, and the area of that circle is (if pi = 22/7) exactly 12! or the numbers 1 to 12 multiplied together, or 1 × 2 × 3 × 4 × 5 × 6 × 7 × 8 × 9 × 10 × 11 × 12. Thus, the twelve base numbers of duodecimal arithmetic are included together within a simple geometrical figure that develops naturally from number itself.

This scheme is not an artificial contrivance made up of arbitrarily chosen "sacred numbers." It is entirely natural, being nothing other than the order inherent in the preexistent field of number itself, represented by the twelve base numbers that constitute its essence. The common perception of all ages, of philosophers and scientists alike, is that number is "the first paradigm," the purest, most abstract rational image of the creator's mind, informing every product of nature and framing the relationships between all things. The basic codification of number shown here is, therefore, the ideal expression of the ideal cosmos.

Since it is a natural, preexistent scheme, it may be discovered by anyone at any time who investigates the properties of number. Its discovery has the force of a revelation, for it reveals the underlying order in the numerical cosmos and provides the model for a corresponding order in human affairs.

Myths of cultural origins commonly begin with revelation. A god or goddess imparts the secrets of divine harmony and order to a man who either is or becomes ruler, and he is empowered to codify this knowledge, adopt it as the lawful standard, and reform society in accordance with its principles. This is the myth of the first sacred king and lawgiver.

The first, divinely inspired ruler corresponds to Plato's philosopher-king. Whether as ruler of an individual ordered mind or of an actual community, he governs an ideal realm. It is the terrestrial paradise associated with the Grail and other such talismans of enchantment, a country and people so arranged as to reflect the order of the heavens. It may last for a very long time, but nothing that is created can avoid decay, and in the course of time it either lapses into decadence and dissolution or is destroyed by outside forces.

Yet the idea of a divinely governed earth, and the corresponding idea of a perfectly centered and balanced human mind, are archetypal and influence every movement toward cultural and spiritual renewal. Revelation is always imminent, and on the very rare occasions when it occurs in just the right circumstances, at the right time, to the person who is qualified and able to act usefully upon it—a philosopher-king, no less—the cosmologically ordered nation may actually come into being.

The contents of this revelation are always the same, and the same numerical structure occurs in the image of an ideal city that the revelation brings to mind. In evidence of this are the universal records of nations formed on the same cosmological principles, based on the same code of number, and with the same elaborately hierarchical, ritualized, solar-centered constitution. A constant fundamental code of law, equated with the unchanging pole of the universe, governs these nations. Its images are everywhere apparent, from the centrally placed pillar in the temple within the national sanctuary to the central household hearth, and its chief symbol is the sacred, divinely empowered king, who transmits vitality to the nation and ritually maintains the heavenly order as reflected in the organization of his kingdom.

In all these cases, the nation is divided from its center into four quarters and twelve tribes, with one of the twelve gods and twelve zodiacal powers governing each section, with a circuit of sacred festivals progressing month by month around the whole country in the course of a year, and with a central, national assembly as the annual climax.

Wherever and whenever it occurs, this structured form of society has clearly been drawn from the same original model. The numerical and geometric basis of that original is shown here in the diagrams. Its reappearance at different times is traditionally attributed to revelation, but it may also of course be transmitted—urged upon rulers by missionary philosophers or brought in by new settlers.

Of the countries that have here been examined, those whose first settlers were the Norsemen—Faroe and Iceland—received through their constitutions the pure imprint of tenth-century Scandinavian cosmology. Iceland's constitution, with its four quarters and twelve Thing districts, was essentially the same as that of ancient Ireland, but there was one obvious difference. Whereas in the old Celtic system the pinnacle of the state hierarchy was the High King, the Viking settlers had no supreme ruler, and their state systems were carefully designed to exclude such a figure. In his place was the lawman, an official with no political or executive powers, presiding over a council of representatives from the various Thing districts. The constitution was still based on sovereignty, but exercised collectively rather than by an individual ruler.

This collective form of sovereignty was a later development from the archaic form of sacred kingship. In Mediterranean lands, kings gave way to ruling councils whose members were drawn equally from the twelve tribes of a typical Greek amphictyony. The period of transition was before the sixth century BC. Celtic countries, however, retained the tradition of kingship to the end, in the case of Ireland, up to the twelfth century, when the last High King was deposed by the Normans. There were many Celts, from Ireland and northern Britain, among the early settlers of Iceland, but their influence is not apparent in the state system that the Icelanders adopted. The Viking colonists brought their traditions from Norway, and the Norse culture, according to its myths and legends, was derived from ancient Greece.

In trying to find the origins of a culture and the sequence in which it passed from one race to another, one is notoriously open to delusion. The history of theories about Aryan and other supposedly culture-giving peoples illustrates this well enough. All the examples of ritually structured, pole-centered societies examined in this book must certainly have had some form of common origin, but there is no firm basis for deciding which came first or where they found their common prototype. In the case of all traditional cultures—Celtic, Norse, Greek, and Asian—their sources are unknown and there is not much point in speculating on the subject.

A vast amount of scholarship has been devoted to the search for origins, the cradle of civilization and the pattern of its diffusion around the world. The question has never been resolved, nor can it be, for it is not the right question. The occurrence of similar, cosmologically based societies in Ireland, Scandinavia, Greece, and elsewhere is not explained by a common, geographical place of origin, but by the influence of a constant religious doctrine based on a scientific cosmology.

Behind every example of the twelve-tribe social structure lies that same combination of an all-inclusive, divinely-centered world picture, a religious philosophy that guided toward initiation, and a fundamental code of number on which all institutions were based. Whether renewed by revelation or transmitted from one priesthood to another, this sacred science has made its appearance in all ages and continents, and always with the same effect, the appearance of the idealistic, ritualized form of society, designed in every detail to imitate the cosmos.

It is very rare for a society of this kind to come into being, and today it would hardly be possible. The freedom, seclusion, and protection from corrupting influences that it requires are not available in the modern world. The knowledge that creates it, however, is not just the model for an ideal social organism. Interpreted rightly, it is also the model for the perfectly balanced, centered mind, and in that sense Plato referred to it in the *Republic*. It is, he said, the "heavenly pattern" and that "whoever cares to can perceive and can establish it in their own hearts."

Speaking further of that heavenly pattern and the sacred science illustrated by it, Plato promises that it is worth giving a lifetime to acquiring it, and whoever does so draws blessings to himself and to the place and time in which he lives. If you are not so inclined, he continues, the second best course is simply to have faith in God, for, on his word as a philosopher, "things are taken care of far better than you could possibly imagine."

BIBLIOGRAPHY

I Finding the Center

Allcroft, A. Hadrian. *The Circle and the Cross.* London, 1927. Vol. 1 on moots, Things, assemblies at prehistoric sites; see esp. geographical centrality of Stonehenge and Celtic ritual sites, 1, 298–300.

Cook, A. B. *Zeus, a Study in Ancient Religion.* London, 1940. The omphalos.

Eitel, Ernest J. *Feng-Shui, or The Rudiments of Natural Science in China.* Hong Kong, 1873. Reprint, London, 1984. Chinese geomancy and the ritual planning of landscapes and buildings.

Eliade, Mircea. *Images et symbols.* Paris, 1952. Chap. 1, the symbolic center.

———. *Cosmos and History.* New York, 1954. Symbolism of the center, 12–17.

———. *The Sacred and the Profane.* New York, 1959. Sacred space and the world center; see esp. chap. 1, the Achilpa and their pole, 32–36.

———. *Shamanism.* Princeton, 1964. The house pillar or tent pole as world center, 260–66; shamanic ascent, 487–94.

———. *Myths, Rites, Symbols.* New York, 1975. Symbols of the center, 377–82.

Godwin, Joscelyn. *Arktos: the Polar Myth in Science, Symbolism, and Nazi Survival.* London and Michigan, 1993.

Gomme, George L. *Primitive Folk-Moots or Open-Air Assemblies in Britain.* London, 1880. The London Stone and Jack Cade, 155–56.

Harrison, Jane E. *Epilegomena to the Study of Greek Religion and Themis.* New York, 1962. The omphalos, 369–415.

Le Roux, Francoise, and Christian J. Guyonvarc'h. *Les Druides.* Ouest-France, 1986. The Celtic center, the high king, Mediolanum and Drunemeton, 217–28.

Lethaby, W. R. *Architecture, Mysticism and Myth.* London, 1892. At the centre of the earth, Chapter IV; the world's centre, Chapter VIII.

———. *Architecture, Nature and Magic.* London, 1956. Cosmology and architecture.

MacGregor, Alasdair Alpin. *Skye and the Inner Hebrides.* London, 1953. The pole of MacDuffie, 205.

Michell, John, and Christine Rhone. *Twelve-Tribe Nations and the Science of Enchanting the Landscape.* London: Thames and Hudson, 1992.

Perry, John W. *Lord of the Four Quarters.* New York, 1966. Kingship, the axial center, and the cosmological order, 3–33.

Plato. *Laws.* Book V, the cosmological city, 656–57.

Raglan, Lord. *The Temple and the House.* London, 1964. Chap. IX, the hearth fire.

Richer, Jean. *Geographie sacrée do monde grec.* Paris, 1983. Astrological divisions of classical landscapes.

Roscher, W. H. *Omphalos.* Leipzig, 1852.

Spencer, Baldwin, and F. J. Gillen. *The Arunta: A Study of a Stone Age People.* London: Macmillan, 1927.

Tompkins, Peter. *Secrets of the Great Pyramid.* London, 1973. Akhenaten, his central capital, and the geodetic system of ancient Egypt, in Appendix by L. C. Stecchini, 336–45.

Warren, Dr. W. F. *Paradise Found.* Boston, 1885. Ancient cosmology, mythical geography, and human origins at the North Pole.

2 The Northern Isles

Balfour, David, ed. *Oppressions of the Sixteenth Century in the Islands of Orkney and Zetland.* Edinburgh, 1859. Tingwall Law Holm, 36–37.

Crawford, Barbara E. *Scandinavian Scotland.* Leicester, England, 1987. Thing sites, 206; views of Tingwall Holm and Finlaggan, figs. 77, 79.

Fenton, Alexander. *The Northern Isles: Orkney and Shetland.* Edinburgh, 1978. Thing of Fetlar, 69–70.

Goundie, Gilbert. *The Celtic and Scandinavian Antiquities of Shetland.* Edinburgh and London, 1904. Tingwall Law Holm, 93, 146, 230.

Grant, I. F. *The Lordship of the Isles.* Edinburgh and London, 1935.

Hibbert, Dr. Samuel. "Tings of Orkney and Shetland." *Archaeologia Scotia* (Journal of the Society of Antiquaries of Scotland) 111 (1831): 103–210.

———. *A Description of the Shetland Isles.* Edinburgh, 1822.

Low, George. *A Tour through the Islands of Orkney and Shetland, 1774.* Kirkwall, 1879. Things, 77, 156.

Martin, Martin. *A Description of the Western Isles of Scotland.* London, 1703.

Munro, R. W. *Monro's Western Isles of Scotland.* London, 1961. The Council of the Isles, records of the lordship, and Loch Finlaggan, 95–110.

Nelson, G. M. *The Story of Tingwall Kirk.* Edinburgh, 1965.

Pálsson, Hermann, and Paul Edwards, trans. *Orkneyinga Saga.* London, 1978. Vikings draw a boat across the neck of Kintyre, 86.

Repp, T. G. *A Historical Treatise on Trial by Jury, Wager of Law . . . in Scandinavia and Iceland.* Edinburgh, 1832. The Thing, 47–52.

Schei, Liv Kjørsvik, and Gunnie Moberg. *The Shetland Story.* London, 1988.

Swire, O. F. *The Inner Hebrides and their Legends.* Glasgow and London, 1964. Loch Finlaggan and the inauguration stone, 175–76.

3 Why the Alting Met at Tórshavn

Dasent, Sir George W. *The Story of Burnt Njal.* Introduction. London, 1900. The Icelandic constitution, administrative divisions, local Things and procedures at the Al-thing.

Du Chaillu, Paul B. *The Viking Age.* London, 1889. Sites and customs of the Thing, chap. XXXVII.

Erlingsson, Thorstein. *Ruins of the Saga Time.* London, 1899. Icelandic Thing sites described and illustrated.

Jones, Prudence. *A "House" System from Viking Europe.* Cambridge, 1991. Astrological divisions of time and territory.

Mallet, Paul H. *Northern Antiquities.* London, 1898. Supplementary chapter by I. A. Blackwell on the foundation and constitution of Iceland, 276–309.

Pálsson, Einar. *The Dome of Heaven.* Reykjavik, 1982.

———. *Celtic Christianity in Pagan Iceland.* Reykjavik, 1985.

———. *The Roots of Icelandic Culture.* Reykjavik, 1986. A summary in English of seven volumes, published in Icelandic.

———. *Pythagoras and Early Icelandic Law.* Reykjavik, 1993. The latest in Pálsson's *oeuvre* locates the origin of Iceland's foundation law and traditions in the esoteric number code of ancient Greece and the Near East.

Schei, Liv Kjørsvik, and Connie Moberg. *The Faroe Islands.* London, 1991. Sandur church and ting, 218–20; Oravik Ting, 232.

Swaney, Deanna. *Iceland, Greenland and the Faroe Islands.* Hawthorn, Australia, 1991. An historical and topographical guide.

Young, G. V. C. *From the Vikings to the Reformation: A Chronicle of the Faroe Islands up to 1538.* Douglas, 1979. Early history of Tinganes and the Ting system of Faroe.

4 The Center of the Isle of Man

Broderick, G., trans. *Chronicle of the Kings of Man.* Edinburgh, 1973.

Cowell, Thomas M. *Baldwin My Valley.* Isle of Man, 1989. St. Luke's Church, Keeill Abban, 43–51.

Craine, David. *Manannan's Isle.* Douglas, Isle of Man, 1955. Manx constitution and sheading courts.

Cubbon, W. *The Treen Divisions of Man.* Douglas, Isle of Man, 1937.

———. *Island Heritage.* Manchester, 1952. Divisions of the Western Isles, chap 9.

Farrant, R. D. *Mann. Its Land Tenure, Constitution, Lords Rent and Deemsters.* Oxford and London, 1937. The author was First Deemster of the Isle of Man.

Marstrander, Carl. "The Keill and the Treen." Oslo, 1938. A typescript translation from the Norwegian is in the Manx Museum in Douglas, and a summary was published in *The Manx Museum Journal* IV (54), March 1938. Manx land divisions and their antiquity.

Stenning, E. H. *Portrait of the Isle of Man.* London, 1958.

Talbot, Rev. T. *The Manorial Roll of the Isle of Man.* Oxford, 1924. 1511–15.

Train, Joseph. *A Historical Account and Statistical Survey of the Isle of Man.* Douglas, Isle of Man, 1845.

Young, G. V. C. *Now Through a Glass Darkly: The History of the Isle of Man under the Norse.* Peel, 1981.

———. *A Brief History of the Isle of Man.* Peel, Isle of Man, 1983.

5 A Diversion to the Center of England

Agutter, Doreen M. K. *Meriden: Its People and Houses.* Two parts. Birmingham, 1990, 1992. The Meriden Cross as England's center and the Cyclists' Memorial, pt. 1, 1.

Arden-Close, Sir Charles. "The Centres of England and Wales." *The Geographical Journal* (1941): 178–81. Royal Geographical Society, London. Methods of finding the geographical center applied to Britain.

Banks, F. R. *Warwickshire and the Shakespeare Country.* Harmondsworth, 1960. A Penguin guide; Meriden and the Woodmen of Arden, 125–27.

Blight, John T. *A Week at the Land's End.* London, 1861. Sancreed Church and its dedication, 170–72.

Burgess, J. Tom. *Historic Warwickshire.* London, 1876. Earliest known reference to Meriden as England's center, the tree at Leamington, High Cross, 16–19.

Cornish, Vaughan. *Historic Thorn Trees in the British Isles.* London, 1941. Thorn trees as central landmarks and assembly places, the Salcombe Regis Thorn, 66–74.

Guest, Lady Charlotte, trans. *The Mabinogion.* London, 1849. In the story "Llud and Llefelys," Oxford is discovered to be the center of England.

Pennick, Nigel. *The Ancient Science of Geomancy.* London, 1979.

———. *The Cosmic Axis.* Cambridge, 1987. Central landmarks in Britain and Europe.

Trubshaw, Bob. *The Quest for the Omphalos.* Loughborough, 1991.

Stukeley, William. *Itinerarium Curiosum.* London, 1724. High Cross illustrated.

6 The Center of Ireland

Best, R., trans. "The Settling of the Manor of Tara." In *Ériu.* IV, 1910.

Cambrensis, Giraldus. Wright, T., trans. *Topographia Hiberniae.* London, 1905. Stone at the navel of Ireland, 117.

Dames, Michael. *Mythic Ireland.* London, 1992. Mide, Uisnech, the center of Ireland, folklore, and geographical observations, 194–245.

Ellis, Peter Berresford. *Celtic Inheritance.* London, 1985. The Druidic social order, 4–21; ancient Ireland, 81–98.

———. *A Dictionary of Irish Mythology.* Oxford, 1991.

English, N. W. "Kilkenny West Pinnacle." *Journal of the Old Athlone Society* 1 (2) (1970–1971). Account of the pinnacle and other reputed centers of Ireland.

Guénon, René. *The Lord of the World (Le roi du monde).* 1927. Reprint, Yorkshire, 1983. The world-center and the mystical ruler, cosmological division of Ireland, 54–55.

Keating, Geoffrey, ed., and D. Comyn, trans. *The History of Ireland.* London, 1902–14. A 16th-century compilation, originally in Irish, of history, lore, and legends.

Macalister, R. A. S., ed. and trans. *Lebor Gabála Erenn.* Dublin, 1938–41.

Macalister, R. A. S., and R. L. Praeger. "Report on the Excavations at Uisneach." In *Proceedings of the Royal Irish Academy* 38c (1928–29).

MacNeill, Eoin. *Celtic Ireland.* Dublin and London, 1921. History, legends, genealogies, ancient literature, and the political and social framework of ancient Ireland, 58.

O'Brien, Gearoid. ("Oisin") "The Centre of Ireland." *The Westmeath Independent,* December 27, 1991.

Rees, Alwyn, and Brinley Rees. *Celtic Heritage.* London, 1961. Cosmological divisions of Ireland, the hierarchy of provinces, the center in Irish and universal tradition, pt. 2, 83–186.

Robertson, Ian. *Blue Guide: Ireland.* London, 1989. The center of Ireland, 261.

Thorpe, Lewis, trans. *The History of the Kings of Britain by Geoffrey of Monmouth.* London, 1966. Merlin moves the Giants' Ring from Mount Killaraus (Killare at the Hill of Uisnech) in Ireland and sets it up at Stonehenge, 196–98.

Smyth, Daragh. *A Guide to Irish Mythology.* Dublin, 1988.

Weir, Hugh W. L., ed. *Ireland: a Thousand Kings.* County Clare, 1989. Essays on Ireland and royalty.

Woods, James. *Annals of Westmeath, Ancient and Modern.* Dublin, 1907. Antiquities and traditions of Uisneach, 239–50.

SOURCES OF
ILLUSTRATIONS

1. Photo of the monument near Lebanon, Kansas, set up in 1939 to mark the geographical center of the United States.
2. The official geographical center of South America, western Brazil. Photo, Keith Payne.
4. Map of Peloponnesus. After *William Hughes Philips' Handy Classical Atlas,* 1906.
5. Map of Celtic Gaul. After *William Hughes Philips' Handy Classical Atlas,* 1906.
6. Law Holm, Loch of Tingwall, Shetland. Photo, Neil Anderson.
7. Map of the Law Ting Holm, Loch of Tingwall, Shetland.
9. Map of the Shetland Isles, from "The Thing Sites of Orkney & Shetland" in *Archaeologia Scotia,* 1831, by Dr. Samuel Hibbert.
13. Macdonald of the Isles, from *The Clans of the Scottish Highlands,* by James Logan, 1845.
15. Map of the Council Island from *Monro's Western Isles,* by R. W. Munro, 1961. Crown copyright reserved.
16. Tinganes at Tórshavn, Faroe Islands. Photo copyright Graeme G. Storey, Shetland.
17. Map of the Faroe Islands. Copyright Geodaetisk Institut, 1983.
18. The four ritual divisions of Iceland, after S. Sturluson, *Heimskringla,* 1932.
19. Drawing of Icelandic hall from *Ruins of the Sagas* by Thorstein Erlingsson, 1899.

20. Al-thing site, Thingvellir, Iceland. Early 18th century drawing.
21. A doom ring, Arnesthing, from *Ruins of the Sagas* by Thorstein Erlingsson, 1899.
22. The three-legged symbol of Manannan.
23. Map of the British Isles, after William R. Shepherd, *Historical Atlas,* 1929.
24. John "Warwick" Smith, *St John's on Tynwald Day,* copyright 1795. Watercolor. Photo, Manx National Heritage.
25. John "Warwick" Smith, *Tynwald Mound,* copyright 1795. Watercolor. Photo, Manx National Heritage.
27. Map of the Isle of Man, after Ordnance Survey, 1873.
28. Edward Henry Corbould, *King Orry the Dane,* copyright 1850. Watercolor. Photo, Manx National Heritage.
29. St Luke's Church, Isle of Man, 1836. Lithograph after a drawing by Captain Wallace. Photo, Manx National Heritage.
30. Stone for a king's foot. Photo, Manx National Heritage.
31. View southward from the Tynwald Mound at Keeill Abban, Isle of Man. Photo, Annabelle Conyngham.
32. View northward from St Luke's Church, Isle of Man. Photo, Annabelle Conyngham.
33. Map showing the alignment of St Luke's Church and the four quarter-land farmsteads, after Ordnance Survey, 1870.
35. Postcard of Meriden Cross, Warwickshire, copyright 1910. Photo, Coventry City Libraries.
36. Map of Roman Britain, after *Encyclopaedia Britannica,* 1911.
37. High Cross and the border between Leicestershire and Warwickshire. Drawing from *Itinerarium Curiosum* by William Stukeley, 1724.
38. Midland Oak, the oak tree at Lillington, Warwickshire, from *Picturesque Warwickshire* by W. S. Brassington, 1906.
40. Celtic cross and Sancreed Church, Cornwall, from *A Week at The Land's End* by S. T. Blight, 1876.
41. Eoin Concannon, last king of the Claddagh. Photo, Tom Kenny.
42. The Stone of Divisions, Uisnech. Photo, Seaver Leslie.

47. Map showing the claimed centers of Ireland, after Ordnance Survey, 1857–77.

The following illustrations are by Christine Rhone: 3, 8, 10, 11, 12, 14, 26a–b, 34, 39, 43, 44, 45, 46, 48a–b, 49, 50a–d, 51.

INDEX

Page numbers in *italics* refer to the captions.

Books of Related Interest

The Dimensions of Paradise
Sacred Geometry, Ancient Science, and the Heavenly Order on Earth
by John Michell

Twelve-Tribe Nations
Sacred Number and the Golden Age
by John Michell and Christine Rhone

Sacred Number and the Origins of Civilization
The Unfolding of History through the Mystery of Number
by Richard Heath

Matrix of Creation
Sacred Geometry in the Realm of the Planets
by Richard Heath

The Return of Sacred Architecture
The Golden Ratio and the End of Modernism
by Herbert Bangs, M.Arch.

The Genesis and Geometry of the Labyrinth
Architecture, Hidden Language, Myths, and Rituals
by Patrick Conty

The Temple of Man
by R. A. Schwaller de Lubicz

The Temple in Man
Sacred Architecture and the Perfect Man
by R. A. Schwaller de Lubicz

INNER TRADITIONS • BEAR & COMPANY
P.O. Box 388
Rochester, VT 05767
1-800-246-8648
www.InnerTraditions.com

Or contact your local bookseller